W9-AXH-953

DISCARD

BOOKS BY KRISTI D. HOLL

Just Like a Real Family
Mystery by Mail
Footprints Up My Back
The Rose Beyond the Wall
First Things First
Cast a Single Shadow
Perfect or Not, Here I Come

Perfect or Not,
Here I Come

JF

Perfect or Not, Here I Come

KRISTI D. HOLL

Jay County Public Library
Portland, Indiana

ATHENEUM   1986   NEW YORK

Copyright © 1986 by Kristi D. Holl

All rights reserved. No part of this book may be reproduced
or transmitted in any form or by any means, electronic or
mechanical, including photocopying, recording, or by any
information storage and retrieval system, without
permission in writing from the publisher.

Atheneum
Macmillan Publishing Company
866 Third Avenue, New York, NY 10022

Type set by Maryland Linotype, Baltimore, Maryland
Printed and bound by Fairfield Graphics, Fairfield, Pennsylvania
Designed by Marjorie Zaum

10 9 8 7 6 5 4 3 2 1

Library of Congress Cataloging-in-Publication Data

Holl, Kristi.   Perfect or not, here I come.

SUMMARY: Life may not be fair, but Tara, seeking
justice, finds how to make the best of things.
I. Title.
PZ7.H7079Pe   1986   [Fic]   86-3605
ISBN 0-689-31284-9

To Karen Whitaker,
the best sister a girl ever had

Contents

Perfect or Not,
Here I Come

1

Drama Night

With her sweaty bangs plastered to her forehead, Tara Brown leaned into the curve. Her muscular legs glided smoothly as she pulled out to pass Amber for the third time.

"Move aside, slowpoke!" she called, grinning. "Here I come again!"

Music swelled over the roller rink's loudspeakers as Tara drew alongside her best friend. Without warning, Amber flung out her arms and crashed to the floor, hitting Tara's ankle. Two seconds later Tara was sprawled on top of her friend.

"You make a good cushion," Tara snorted. Crawling off Amber, she glided smoothly to the edge of the rink. "Come on," she called. "Let's sit this song out."

"Help!" Amber cried from the middle of the rink.

"I'll get killed out here!" Every time she tried to stand, another skater whizzed by, barely missing her fingers.

Tara watched for a break in the Saturday afternoon crowd, then yelled, "Now! Move it!"

Arms flailing, Amber scrambled to her feet and wobbled to where Tara sat. Plopping down on the carpeted edge, she wiped her face on the tail of her shirt. "How'd you ever talk me into learning to roller-skate? What a mob out there! I almost—"

"No loafing around here, girls," came a laughing voice from above them.

Tara glanced up into her teacher's face. "Hi, Miss Dalton. I didn't see you here today."

"Good exercise, especially in this rotten weather. I get cabin fever every February, with the blizzards and ice storms." She ran long fingers through her black curls. "You're not done skating, are you?"

"Just resting," Amber said, leaning back on her elbows. "Tara's working me to death. I just want to relax and massage my crushed elbows."

"*Couples only,*" announced the D.J. into the microphone. Then a deafening song with a throbbing beat blared over the loudspeaker.

Miss Dalton held out her hands. "Anybody want to skate doubles?"

Tara elbowed Amber, who was counting the change from her pocket. "Want to?"

"No, you go ahead. I'm starving." Amber turned toward the concession stand. "Meet you back here after this song," she called over her shoulder.

"Guess it's just you and me." Miss Dalton grasped Tara's hands and they joined the couples rolling counterclockwise around the rink. "Not too fast, please. Today's the first time I've skated in a while."

Tara nodded, pleased to be singled out by her young sixth grade teacher. Until this year, Tara had firmly believed teachers belonged in the same category as parents —stuffy and impossible to please. But after six months in Constance Dalton's room, she'd been forced to change her mind.

Some teachers, at least, could be fun. Miss Dalton was certainly the only teacher Tara knew who spent Saturday afternoons roller-skating.

A young couple in matching T-shirts cruised past them. The girl faced backward, her feet in perfect step with her partner's.

Miss Dalton pointed at them. "Could we do that, maybe?"

"I can't skate backwards," Tara admitted, swaying to the left with her teacher. "Can you?"

"I don't know. I never tried." Miss Dalton grinned down from where she topped Tara's height by only six inches. "Let's give it a shot."

Tara wrinkled her nose. "Only if you do the backward skating." She didn't intend to fall on her fanny in front of all these kids if she could help it.

Miss Dalton guided her to the far end of the rink, out of the main flow of skaters. "I'll try not to trip you. Let's see, on the count of four, you lead with your left foot, and I'll start backward with my right." She took a deep breath and winked. "Ready?"

Tara glanced over her shoulder. "I guess so. Here goes." She nodded her head in time with the music. "One. Two. Three, and *four*."

She pushed off with her left foot while Miss Dalton stepped backward with her right. They skated seven steps before the first turn. Tara leaned into the curve, but her teacher didn't.

Abruptly, their feet locked. For two frantic seconds, Tara grabbed at Miss Dalton, trying to keep her balance. Then, with a gasp, she hit the floor, whacking her elbow on the cement.

Groaning, Tara turned to see if Miss Dalton was hurt, but her teacher was already crawling to her feet. "I guess you don't learn anything new without falling on your face a few times." She reached out to Tara. "Ready to try again?"

Hoping no one had noticed their spill, Tara took Miss Dalton's hands again. She wished they could just skate forward around the rink. But it was like Miss Dalton to try something different, even if they looked like fools doing it.

"One. Two. Three. *Four.*" Miss Dalton stepped back, pulling Tara with her.

This time they made it halfway around the rink before they locked skates and toppled over, and by the time the song ended, they had managed to skate completely around the rink twice without tripping. Congratulating themselves, they headed to where Amber sat munching popcorn.

"Guess I'd better get home." Miss Dalton relaxed next to Amber and removed her skates. "I still have science tests to grade before Monday and I haven't even started. Kids aren't the only ones who hate homework." She stood and flexed her fingers. "See you both Monday." With a wave, she headed toward the exit.

"Bye." Tara sank to the carpet next to her best friend, taking a handful of yellow popcorn from the box Amber held out. "You know," she said, "Miss Dalton is more fun than some kids."

On Monday morning Tara and Amber raced down the school hallway, late again. Tara fumed under her breath. She didn't know why she waited for Amber anymore. At least once a week she made them tardy. Amber just couldn't get excited about getting to school on time.

Sliding to a halt, Tara peeked around the corner of their sixth grade room, where noisy groups of kids milled around. "I think we can sneak in. Come on," she whispered. Tara shook her head as Amber dropped to her knees and crawled into the classroom. "Cute, Amber. Real cute."

Miss Dalton was nowhere in sight. Gratefully, Tara dumped her books on her desk and slid into her seat. Karin Allen promptly knocked the books off as she stomped by, holding two squeaky mice that belonged in their science maze.

Tara wondered where Miss Dalton was. Richard Weston, a wad of chewing gum like a marble in his cheek, sat with his green boots propped up on the teacher's desk. He gripped a pencil between his teeth, puffing noisily, then blew imaginary smoke rings to the ceiling. Tara read the words on his T-shirt: "It's Hard to be Humble when You Know You're GREAT."

"Here comes the teach!" Amber hissed.

Down came the green feet. The pencil was flipped into Miss Dalton's pencil holder. The two mice, Limburger and Swiss, were whisked into their cage. Groups broke up and kids drifted to their seats.

"Hi, kids. Sorry I'm late." Miss Dalton swept down the aisle to her desk. "Before the first reading group leaves for Miss Button's room, I want to discuss an important event coming up."

The chattering in the back of the room stopped. All Tara could hear was the soft *pop* of Richard blowing a bubble.

"As many of you know, each spring my class produces a play written by a sixth grader. Any interested student in this room may enter a play in the competition. The winning play will be performed by our class on Drama Night."

Beverly Roth's manicured hand shot into the air. "Miss Dalton? Do we have to write a play in order to act on Drama Night?" She flung her waist-length blond hair over her shoulder.

"No, you don't."

Richard popped another bubble, this time louder. Miss Dalton sighed. "Richard, the gum, please."

Grinning, Richard loped to the front of the room. With a long low whistle, he shot his gum into the wastebasket. "*I'll* write a play. How about *The Bubble Gum Bomber?*"

Raising one eyebrow, Miss Dalton simply waited while Richard bounced an invisible basketball back to his desk. "As I started to say, the subject of your play can be any historical period we've studied so far."

Questions came from all parts of the room. "How long does it have to be?" "Do we have to make costumes?" "Who comes to this play, anyway?"

Scrunching down in her seat, Tara smiled to herself.

She already knew all the answers to their questions. Her older sister, Melanie, had had Miss Dalton two years ago, and Tara had pumped Melanie for inside information about the play.

Tara had known for years that *she* wanted to be a playwright some day. The Sixth Grade Drama Night could be her first chance to have a play produced. More importantly, *if* her play was chosen, it was sure to impress her parents. For those reasons, she'd been working on several play ideas since the beginning of the school year.

Miss Dalton raised one finger. "Listen up. When thinking of a topic, keep these things in mind." She listed each point on the blackboard. "Choose an incident in history with lots of *action*. Have at least *six* characters in your play. You need lots of *dialogue* for the speaking parts."

Beverly stroked her long hair. "How about using the Revolutionary War?" she asked, waving her brush in the air.

"The whole war's a bit much for a play this size," Miss Dalton said. "But you could choose one or two incidents from that war to write about."

"Well, then, how about John Smith and Pocahontas?" Beverly asked, shaking her long mane. "Of course, we'd need someone with long hair to braid for the romantic part of Pocahontas."

- "Oh, brother," groaned Oliver Steel. "I'd choose something exciting—like the bombing of Pearl Harbor."

"Or when Lincoln gets shot at Ford Theater," piped up Amber.

"Or the Forty-Niners and the Gold Rush."

"Or when—"

Miss Dalton waved her arms, interrupting them. "You've got the right idea. Those not acting in the play will help with scenery, costumes, programs, and ushering. We'll talk about it more later." She headed to the back of the room, ruffling Richard's hair as she passed his desk. "The first reading group can go next door to Miss Button's room now."

Some of Miss Button's students were already straggling into the room where Miss Dalton taught science and social studies for both sixth grades. Her voice rose over the shuffling feet. "Those of you in science can get your coats. We'll go outside to test your weather instruments this morning."

Tara trudged out the door with her reading and spelling books. Although she loved to read, she hated going to the other room.

Old Miss Button was a drill sergeant. She marched up and down the aisles with a ruler, ready to crack the knuckles of anyone who dared whisper. Each student stood and recited in turn, but wasn't allowed to talk the rest of the hour. Tara loved getting back to Miss Dalton's class. Something neat was always happening there.

The rest of the day Tara mulled over her ideas for Drama Night. Later that afternoon, at home in her room, Tara pulled her dog-eared notebook from the center drawer of her desk.

"Melanie'd better be right about Miss Dalton's favorite time being the Civil War period," she muttered.

For the past several months Tara had made detailed notes on the Civil War. The time had come to decide which part to develop into her play. Tara figured it was sure to help her chances to choose her teacher's favorite time in history.

Tara curled up on her bed, poring over the notes she'd made from library books. She'd learned about little known battle plans from *The Civil War: Strange & Fascinating Facts*. She'd studied about slavery in *The Illustrated History of the Civil War*.

Tara paced around her room, trying to remember the discussion that day in school. "The other kids will probably write about battles like Bunker Hill, or famous people like Columbus or George Washington," she muttered, staring hard at her reflection in the wall mirror. "I need something different, something different . . ."

Snapping her fingers, she dashed back to her notebook. With a flying leap, she landed on her bed and riffled the pages.

She skimmed the notes she'd collected on the Civil War. Although most of it had been interesting, one particular time had really captured her sympathy.

She flipped two more pages. "Here it is!" She jabbed her finger in the middle of a page. "I bet nobody will choose this to write about, but it's definitely about the Civil War period."

Absent-mindedly chewing on her pencil, Tara read the notes she'd taken on the Underground Railroad. This was the name given to the system that helped smuggle slaves to freedom in the North. It got its name, she read, because "those who took passage on it disappeared from public view as truly as if they'd gone into the ground." She'd write her play about smuggling slaves on the Underground Railroad!

During her research she'd read a lot about life in the Old South. The more she'd read about slavery, the more indignant she'd grown. Imagine—people owning other people, buying and selling them! How could white people of that time think they were so much better than the black people?

Tara shook her head, puzzled. No black families lived in their small Midwestern town. Since she'd never known many black people herself, she was surprised at her own strong reaction to slavery, especially since it was a dead issue. And yet, there was something about it that hit home.

Maybe it was the whole idea that some people thought they were perfect, while another group of people was second-class. Tara'd certainly never been a slave, but she knew from experience how it felt to be treated like a second-class citizen.

She skimmed her notes. "Hmmm, maybe I should check with Melanie and make sure no one's used this idea before," she decided. If she accidentally copied some-one else's old play, she could kiss her chances of winning good-bye.

Dashing down the hall, Tara peeked into Melanie's room. It was empty, so she went on to the bathroom, where Melanie spent most of her time these days. Sure enough, Tara found her in front of the mirror, dental floss strung between two fingers.

"Melanie, I need to ask you something." Tara perched on the edge of the tub.

"Whuh?" Melanie worked around her shiny new braces with the floss.

"Do you remember if anyone ever wrote about the Underground Railroad for Drama Night?"

"Whuh?" Melanie sawed the floss back and forth between her front teeth.

"You know, where Northerners helped slaves escape just before the Civil War." Tara peered into the mirror at her sister. "What are you trying to do?"

Melanie took her hands out of her mouth. "We had tacos for lunch at school. I just know there's a piece of lettuce stuck in there. I can feel it."

Tara shook her head. Ever since Melanie'd gotten her braces a month ago, she spent most of her time flossing her teeth or rinsing her retainer. Gross.

"Well, do you remember if anyone used that subject for their play?"

"I don't remember it, so I guess not."

"Good." Tara raced back down the hall.

Plopping on the bed, she grabbed a dozen sheets of notebook paper. "Scene One," she wrote boldly across the top of the first page. Then, for five minutes, she chewed her pencil lead.

The scenes she wrote would have to have mostly black characters, Tara realized, and there were no black students in her school. Although, with the proper make-up, the slave characters could look authentic, would Miss Dalton think it was too much of a drawback? Maybe. On the other hand, it might be just the topic to interest her tender-hearted teacher. Miss Dalton was always defending some group or other, wanting to give them a fair shake.

Tara nodded. The Underground Railroad might be just the right subject after all.

For the next two hours, she worked feverishly. By suppertime, she'd decided on two dramatic scenes to act out, with a short intermission in between. To set the proper mood, she decided to have a narrator introduce each scene.

Since it was her play, of course she'd be the narrator. Maybe she'd even have music, something scary, to help create the right atmosphere to watch the runaway slaves.

Whistling, she skipped down the stairs two at a time and headed for the dining room. The play was already beginning to come alive in her mind.

She took a deep breath. "I just *know* this is going to be my big break," she whispered to herself.

Tara could picture it easily: the authentic costumes, the realistic scenery, the dramatic performance. Her parents would sit proudly in the front row, love and approval written on their faces.

Thundering applause from an imaginary audience echoed in Tara's head as she slid into her seat at the table.

⚜ 2 ⚜

Tara's Big Break

Tara's eyes were glued to the TV screen. Scarlett O'Hara, squeezing a handful of red Georgia clay, shook her fist at the sky. "As God is my witness, I'll never be hungry again!" she shouted.

With a swell of music, the movie faded to a commercial. Tara and her mom stretched and reached for more popcorn. Tara's mom, who led exercise classes at the Body Boutique, had Saturday off, so she was glad to run her *Gone With the Wind* tape on the VCR for Tara. Her mom loved that movie. Ever since she'd recorded it (absent-mindedly leaving in the commercials), she'd watched it at least once a month.

Tara opened her notebook to a clean page and began to scribble.

"What are you doing?" her mother asked.

"Taking notes. There are slaves in the play I'm writing for school. I want to study Mammy's and Prissy's costumes in this part coming up." Surprised at her mother's interest, Tara smiled shyly. "Also the dialect has to be just right and I thought—"

"Shh-h-h-h-h!" Her mom cut her off abruptly as the commercial ended.

Sighing, Tara sat forward and watched carefully. She'd seen this movie a couple of times the year before. It *was* good, she admitted, glancing at her mother. Still, how could someone be nutty enough to name her children after its characters?

Tara jotted down notes as Mammy waddled across the wide front veranda. " 'You'd be a sight more humil'-ated, Miss Suellen, if Mr. Kennedy's lice gets on ya.' " Frowning, Tara tried to copy Mammy's nineteenth-century dialect exactly.

She also sketched the bandanna tied around Mammy's head and the flapping apron covering her dress. After studying the young slave girl, Prissy, and the house servant, Pork, Tara settled back in her chair. Relaxing, she watched more of the movie as she finished off the bowl of popcorn.

But as the story unfolded, she found herself feeling almost critical of the movie. Even if the details of the slaves' dress and accent were accurate, she had to wonder if the slave conditions were shown realistically. The slaves in the movie seemed so happy, so content with their servant's place in Southern society. But if slaves had been so happy, why had the Underground Railroad sprung up?

Tara picked popcorn hulls out of her teeth. Even if the slaves *had* been content, which she doubted, it still wasn't right. No one should own someone else. No one should have that kind of power over another human being.

She snapped her notebook shut and tiptoed from the room as Scarlett O'Hara, wearing a green velvet dress made from curtains, left to visit the hero, Rhett Butler, in jail.

Coming around the corner of the kitchen, something hard as stone whacked Tara's shin. "Ow! You little creep, what did you hit me with? A rock?"

Tara's second-grade brother, Rhett, yanked his skinny arm back. A green Yo-Yo flew through the air and over his shoulder. "Isn't this neat? I bought it today."

"Watch what you're doing!" Tara rubbed her bruised leg. "You don't throw Yo-Yos, you know."

"I wasn't throwing it. That was a Yo-Yo trick called Around the World." He looped the string over his middle finger. "Dad showed me how to Rock the Cradle and Walk the Dog too."

"Then go walk your dog outside." At the end of the hall, Tara took the stairs three at a time, her notes gripped in her hand. She was anxious to finish the details of her play while the Old South setting was still fresh in her mind.

She met Melanie coming out of the bathroom. Her mouth was all red and stretched-looking.

"You flossing again?" Tara asked. "You're going to saw right through your braces some day."

"I wish I could." Melanie peered over Tara's shoulder. "What's that?"

"Notes from Mom's movie that I need for my play for Drama Night." She leaned against the doorway. "Don't you think it's weird being named for parts of that old movie?"

"I never thought about it much."

"Well, who else has names like ours? Rhett's named after Rhett Butler, you after Melanie Hamilton, and I got stuck with the name of a plantation." Tara lowered her voice to a rumble. " 'The red . . . earth . . . of Tara,' " she intoned.

Melanie burst out laughing. "It could be worse. At least Mom didn't name us Mammy and Prissy!"

"True," Tara agreed. "Hey, could you do me a favor later?"

"What kind of favor?"

"Would you type my play for me on the computer?" Melanie and her mom were the only ones who could type very fast. "I know Mom's too busy, but I wanted my play on a disk so I can print as many copies as we'll need." She paused. "If my play's chosen, that is."

"I guess so." Melanie sighed. "I'm not doing anything else tonight."

Melanie was in eighth grade, but ever since she got braces, she didn't go out with her friends much. It seemed to Tara that her sister spent most of her time at the mirror, examining her mouth.

"Thanks, Mel." Tara ducked into her room and spent the rest of the afternoon revising and reworking her play.

Finally both scenes were as exciting as she could make them. For the intermission, she planned a stirring reading of some Civil War poetry. It would set the tone for the second scene, where Lizzie escaped from the slave catchers across a frozen river. Maybe she could find some rousing Civil War battle songs to be played in the background while she read. *Perfect* atmosphere.

At nine o'clock Melanie presented Tara with a printed copy of her play. She'd even created a title page. "Smuggled to Safety, by Tara Brown" was centered on the cover.

"Hey, this looks neat! Do you think it'll win?"

"It might. It's better than the play *we* did about Lee's surrender. There were just a lot of soldiers lying around covered in fake ketchup blood."

Tara frowned. "Unfortunately, there are two other good writers in my class, Sherman Tool and Vicki Jacobs. They're both writing plays too." Tara clutched her script tight. "I've just *got* to win. Maybe after plays, I'll do movies. Who knows? Maybe I'll do a remake of *Gone With the Wind*! At least Mom would notice *that*."

Melanie tapped the printed pages. "Is getting Mom and Dad's attention the real reason you want to win so bad?"

"You have to admit—it would take something big like this for them to even notice I'm alive." Tara shrugged. "You wouldn't understand, Mel. They think you're perfect."

"No, they don't!"

"Yes, sir! You get straight A's, you're in gifted math and science classes. You know more about running programs on our computer than even Dad does." Tara gripped her play. "Since perfect is all they notice, I'll see to it that this play *is* perfect."

On Monday morning Tara handed in her entry for the competition. Miss Dalton glanced at the cover. "This looks very professional, Tara. I'll be anxious to read it."

"Um, do you know when you might pick the winner?" Tara asked, hoping she sounded casual.

"Since the entries have to be in by Wednesday, I can

announce the winner on Friday." She shook her head at Richard Weston, who was sticking a gooey wad of chewed gum under his desk. "Good luck, Tara."

"Thanks." Turning, Tara spotted Amber waving from the back of the room. She picked her way around the wooden model of America's first railroad that they'd built for social studies class.

Amber made room for Tara on the window ledge where she was perched. "What were you doing up at Miss Dalton's desk?"

"Turning in my play for the competition. Did you get yours done?"

"No time. After my dance lesson on Friday, then a voice lesson on Saturday, I was pooped." Amber bounced on the window ledge, clapping her hands in a complicated rhythm. "I'd rather just perform in the play anyway. You didn't happen to write a musical, did you?"

Tara snorted. "Oh sure!"

When Miss Dalton flipped the light switch off, then back on, they hurried to their desks. Tara dug out her reading and spelling books, but she couldn't stop thinking about her play.

Somehow, she just *had* to win the competition.

The knot in Tara's stomach grew each day. By Friday morning she could barely choke down a pancake for breakfast. Miss Dalton was to announce the winner just before lunch. Tara'd reread her play a dozen times that week. She was convinced it was good—but was it good enough?

At 11:30 that morning Tara looked up from hunting for her lunch ticket. At the front of the room, Miss Dalton held some paper-clipped pages in each hand. Tara knew that one play was hers—she recognized the cover page Melanie had made. She squinted, but couldn't make out the name on the other play. Suddenly Tara's throat felt dry and scratchy, as if it were coated with corn flakes.

"This year, deciding which play to produce was very difficult," Miss Dalton began. "By Wednesday night I'd narrowed it down to two plays, but not until early this morning could I finally choose."

Tara glanced across the room at Vicki Jacobs. She bet the other play was hers. Vicki hardly ever opened her mouth except to say "yes" or "no," but Tara knew she got straight A's in English and Composition. She might look like a scared rabbit, but she could write.

Beverly waved her hairbrush in the air. "So whose play won? Is there a part for someone with long hair?"

Richard blew a giant pink bubble. It popped, covering his chin and half his nose. "Sure it does," he croaked, peeling the gum from his skin. He clutched his throat and, in a gravelly voice, begged, " 'Rapunzel, Rapunzel, let down your hair.' "

Miss Dalton shook her head. "The gum, please, Richard."

She waited in silence while Richard pelted his gum into the wastebasket and returned to his desk. "The two plays were written by Tara Brown and Sherman Tool. Both students chose to write about incidents from the Civil War."

Tara winced. Had Sherman discovered that Miss Dalton loved the Civil War period too? She glanced up the aisle at Sherman, who faced straight ahead, his wire-rimmed glasses smudged over as usual.

"Since I did have to make a choice, I decided we'd produce Tara's play. It's based on the Underground Railroad." Miss Dalton held up Tara's script. "Congratulations, Tara."

Tara's hand jerked, ripping her lunch ticket. "Thanks, Miss Dalton."

Miss Dalton patted Sherman's arm when she handed him his play. "This was very well done, Sherman. Perhaps you could read yours to the class during social studies. I wish we had time to do two plays."

Sherman smiled stiffly. "I didn't think I'd win anyway."

Tara went limp at her desk. It had finally happened —her first big break! All week she'd pictured her play, step by step, in living color. It would be an extravaganza long remembered by Winchester Heights Elementary.

It would be dazzling—with authentic-looking costumes, soft shadowy lighting, eerie sound effects, and realistic make-up. As if born with some instinct, Tara knew exactly how each line should be spoken, how each actor should move across the stage. She gripped her hands tightly together in her lap. She couldn't wait to direct the play as she'd rehearsed it so many times in her mind.

"The Underground Railroad was a system used by Northern sympathizers to smuggle slaves to freedom, usually to Canada," Miss Dalton said as Tara snapped back to attention. "Most of the smuggling was done for free, but Tara has written about John Fairfield, who was slightly different. He received payment from Negroes already in Canada to smuggle away their friends and relatives and bring them up North too."

Beverly yawned delicately. "But who cares?"

Miss Dalton's eyes flashed. "When any part of society is treated so unfairly as the slaves were, we should *all* care," she said firmly. "It's true that our area of the Midwest has few black families, and Winchester Heights has no black students at all. But even though we're isolated in that way, we should still be aware of the history of this segment of our population."

Tara sat forward in surprise. She'd only hoped Miss Dalton would like her play, but she had really hit a nerve.

Miss Dalton surveyed the classroom slowly. "Maybe in learning about something as despicable as slavery, it can be prevented from ever happening again." She smiled slightly and her voice softened. "So, except for John Fairfield and some slave catchers, all the characters in Tara's play are Negroes."

Beverly brushed her long hair, hunting for split ends. "John Fairfield? Aren't there any girls in this play?"

Miss Dalton held up Tara's play. "Yes, there are parts for girls in this play." She handed Tara's script to her. "Perhaps you could tell us about the scenes you've written."

Tara flipped to page one of her play. "Well, in my first scene Fairfield is driving a wagon through some woods, with a slave family hidden in the back. Two slave catchers jump out from behind some trees after the wagon stops for the night. They capture Elijah, the slave father, and Mandy, the daughter. The slave mother, Lizzie, escapes on foot carrying her baby boy."

Beverly jumped up. "I'll take the part of Lizzie!"

"You may certainly read for that part," Miss Dalton agreed. "Tryouts will be after school on Monday."

"I could bring extra copies of the play," Tara volunteered. "Melanie can run off what we need."

"Well, if you're sure, that would be a big help," Miss Dalton said.

Richard tossed a pack of strawberry gum in the air and caught it in his teeth. "What happens in the rest of the play?"

"Um, after a short intermission, the second half tells about Lizzie being chased by the slave catchers." Tara's stomach did a flipflop. For some reason, she felt silly talking about her play to the whole class. "She comes to a frozen river with chunks of ice floating in it. Just before the slave catchers grab her baby, she escapes across the river."

"Neat!" Peter Griffith leaned forward and tapped Tara on the back. "I'll be Fairfield. I could wear a long mustache—one of those handlebar things."

Tara felt her cheeks grow warm. If it were *her* choice, she'd let Peter have any part he wanted. But he was very artistic—she hoped to work closely with him on the scenery.

The lunch bell rang and shoving students surged out the door, turning toward the cafeteria. Amber waited while Tara carefully put away her play.

"Way to go, Tara! I knew you'd win." Leaning close, she whispered, "What did you plan for the intermission?"

"Nothing definite yet. Something that goes with the theme of the play."

"Never fear, Amber's here. I've got a great idea for you." They headed out the door. "How about a tap dance during intermission? While I danced, I could sing 'Way Down upon the Suwannee River.' That's an old southern song."

Tara stared at her best friend. "You've *got* to be

kidding. This is a *drama*. The intermission has to set a serious mood for when Lizzie almost gets caught in the second scene." She kicked an eraser down the hall. "Tap dancing and singing would ruin the whole atmosphere."

"No, it wouldn't. It'd be fun. You don't want everything to be grim."

"Sorry, but it's my play and you're not having a recital at the intermission." Tara shuddered at the thought. "If a tap dance fit the mood of my play, maybe I'd let you do it. But it wouldn't look right."

Amber paused by the front door. She lived just two blocks from school and went home for lunch. "I still think you're wrong. A good song and dance routine would keep everyone awake."

Tara shook her head. Amber wanted to be a performer as much as Tara wanted to produce plays. Tara hoped she'd be a huge success someday too. But Amber wasn't going to ruin Tara's Civil War play to do it.

And that was final.

3

Assistant Director

"But *I* was going to be the director!" Tara protested after lunch. "I know exactly how each scene should be played."

Miss Dalton leaned close and spoke in a low voice. "That's true, but since Sherman's play was runner-up, I thought it'd be fair to let him be the director."

Tara shoved her hair back off her forehead in desperation. She was losing control of her play already. "Can I at least help Sherman? I could be his assistant."

"That might work." Miss Dalton smoothed Tara's ruffled bangs. "You can see what Sherman thinks. We'll have tryouts Monday after school, then begin rehearsals on Tuesday."

Tara breathed a sigh of relief. "Thanks. I'll ask him right now."

Four kids stood in a circle around Sherman's desk. Tara gently nudged Beverly aside. "Guess what, Sherman? You're the director for my play."

Sherman glanced up through his grimy wire rims. "I know. Miss Dalton told me at lunch."

"Oh. Well, anyway, I'm going to be the assistant. When we start rehearsals I can show you exactly what I had in mind for each scene."

"Thanks." Sherman shuffled some papers together.

Tara relaxed, glad that Sherman didn't mind having an assistant. Lots of kids, like Beautiful Beverly, would never share an important job like that.

She glanced at the papers Sherman held. "Is that your play?"

"Yeah, some of the guys wanted to read it." Sherman paper-clipped the pages and slipped them into his desk.

Beverly pulled her hair over one shoulder and braided it. "Some of us thought Sherman's play should have been picked. It's about Lincoln getting shot at Ford Theater. I would probably have played Lincoln's wife, who was with him when it happened."

Her stomach churning, Tara decided to ignore Beverly's crack. "I can see why Miss Dalton had trouble choosing."

Richard fell to one knee and pointed his finger at Sherman. "Bang, bang!" He blew imaginary smoke from the end of his finger. "I'm John Wilkes Booth!" he cried, limping away down the aisle.

Beverly laughed, then turned to Peter Griffith. "Don't you think Sherman's play would be better for Drama Night?"

Peter shrugged and continued to decorate his white tennis shoes with red and green markers. "Both ideas sound good to me."

Beverly pointed the end of her braid at Tara. "Nobody's ever heard of John Fairchild. Who cares what he did anyway?"

"The people who worked in the Underground Railroad were very brave. They . . . struck a blow for freedom. Just ask Miss Dalton," Tara shot back. "And it's Fair*field*, not Fairchild."

Tara had thought the kids would love her play idea. It was something unusual, with lots of action. Of course, Sherman's sounded pretty exciting, too. "Could I read your play too?" she asked him.

He shrugged, then handed Tara his handwritten pages. She couldn't help noticing how professional her printed copy looked in comparison.

As she read Sherman's script about when the actor John Wilkes Booth shot Lincoln, she spotted several places that needed rewriting. By the time she reached the end, the other kids had drifted away.

Straightening the pages, she handed them back.

"This is good, Sherman. I can see why Miss Dalton liked it." She hesitated. Should she tell Sherman why she thought his play had come in second? She was pretty sure she knew. Taking a deep breath, she finally decided it probably wasn't fair *not* to tell him.

"There *were* a couple things I'd change if it were my play."

"Like what?" Sherman added more greasy fingerprints to his glasses.

"Like here." Tara flipped to page three. "All the action happens inside the theater."

"Obviously. That's where Lincoln was shot."

"But to keep the audience interested, you should at least have two different scenes. It's boring, staring at the same set during the whole play." Tara pinched her bottom lip. "I know. You could add the chase scene outside where Booth is captured."

"I hadn't thought of that," Sherman admitted. "That would be more exciting."

Encouraged, Tara added, "There aren't enough speaking lines either. There's too much description in your play." Tara'd studied a few scripts the previous summer at her Y theater class. She knew plays were supposed to be mostly talking. Sherman's play was half stage directions, though. "Concentrate on the dialogue," she advised.

"I'll remember that." Sherman slipped the pages

back into his desk. "If I ever write another play, which I doubt."

"Time for science, Group B." Miss Dalton rolled up her sleeves. "Get out the weather instruments you haven't finished. Try to get done today. Group A has already tested theirs."

From the top storage shelf Tara retrieved her cotton material and plastic hoop. She was making a weather sock like she'd seen at their local airport. The material was sewn into a cone shape, but she still needed to attach the cone to the lightweight hoop.

As she sewed with strong nylon thread, Tara's mind drifted back to her play. What a dream come true! She couldn't wait to tell her parents. And just wait till they came to Drama Night in May. They'd be so proud of her.

By the end of the science hour, Tara's windsock was sewn onto the hoop. She was trying to attach the limp sock to a pole when Miss Dalton flicked the light switch on and off twice, her silent signal to pick up.

Tara stuffed her weather instrument into its shoe box and turned to look for Amber. But she wasn't at her desk or the science shelves, or anywhere else in the room.

At the blackboard, Miss Dalton clapped her hands. "If you didn't—" But her words were cut off when the door at the front of the room flew open with a bang.

Tara's mouth fell open. There in the doorway posed Amber, wearing her blue sequined costume from her last recital. Hands on hips, she took a deep breath and began to sing.

"Way down upon the Suwan*nee* Ri*ver!*" she belted out.

As she sang, she tap-tapped across the room in her black patent leather tap shoes.

"Far, far away . . ." she warbled.

Tap. Tap-tap. Tap. Tap-tap.

"That's where my heart is turn*ing* ev*er!*"

Amber flung her arms wide and paused. "Oops. I forget the rest of the song." Unembarrassed, she tap-tapped back across the room and out the door, waving as she disappeared.

Richard whistled from the back of the room. "More, more!"

"What in the world was that?" Beverly demanded.

Angry, Tara finally closed her gaping mouth. It was just like Amber to pull that, after Tara'd told her absolutely no tap dancing at the intermission.

In less than two minutes, Amber was back from the restroom, her jeans and sweater on. Cheers and whistles filled the air, and she curtsied on the way to her desk.

Miss Dalton's lips twitched. "That was quite a performance," she said. "Any special reason?"

Amber shook her blond hair out of her eyes. "It was an audition, sort of. Wouldn't that be good entertainment for the intermission? 'Suwannee River' is an old southern song, and the dance routine would wake up people who fell asleep during the first half."

"Nobody's going to go to sleep during my play," Tara interrupted. Nobody paid any attention to her.

Karin raised her hand. "I think it's a good idea to have some entertainment during the intermission."

Tara stood up and cleared her throat. "I'd planned a serious poetry reading to set the mood for the second half," she explained, glaring at Amber.

Karin turned to face Tara. "But this dance routine, especially if someone plays the piano, would cover up the noise of scenery being changed behind the curtain."

Miss Dalton nodded. "That's an important consideration, Karin. Well, class, what do you think of Amber's act for the intermission?"

Applause broke out as half the class gave her a standing ovation. "Encore! Encore!" Richard's stomping feet sounded like a bass drum. Miss Dalton grinned at Amber. "I guess that settles it. I'll play the piano for you, if you'd like."

"Thanks, Miss Dalton." Amber bowed solemnly. "I'll learn the rest of the words too."

Beverly leaned near Tara with a smirk. "Guess you're outvoted."

Tara gritted her teeth. "I already told Amber she couldn't tap dance in my play."

"It's not just your play anymore," Beverly hissed. "It's the class play."

Tara slumped back in her seat. "But I wrote it," she muttered.

Glancing at her starry-eyed best friend, Tara tried to stay mad. But Amber's beaming face made it hard. Giving in, Tara decided she couldn't really blame Amber for trying. She wanted to sing and dance as much as Tara wanted to write plays.

That night Tara waited by the back door, anxious to tell her parents about winning the play contest. When she heard their car pull into the driveway, she yanked open the kitchen door.

"Guess what?" she yelled as they climbed out of their shiny car. She hopped from one foot to the other. "I won! I won!"

Tara's mom glanced next door. "For heaven's sake, Tara, stop shouting. What will the neighbors think?"

Biting down on her tongue, Tara stepped back inside as her parents came into the kitchen.

Her dad dumped his briefcase on the counter. "Now, what were you yelling about? What did you win?"

Tara grinned, thrilled to finally have an important announcement to make. "I won the play contest at school. My play is going to be produced on Drama Night!"

"Hey, that *is* great!" Her dad smiled quickly, picked up his briefcase, and clomped down the steps to work at his desk, as he did every night before supper.

Her mom rummaged in the refrigerator for a diet cola. "Did everyone in your class have to write a play?" she asked, popping the top off the can.

"No, just the kids who wanted to."

Her mom held the cold can against her sweaty cheek. "Exactly how many kids *did* you beat out in order to win?"

Tara frowned. "I don't know. What difference does that make?"

"I just wondered if your play was the best out of twenty—or out of four." She poured the pop into a glass. "If your father takes time out of his busy schedule to come to your production, it had better be good."

"It will be!" Shoulders drooping, Tara headed for the stairs, stopping in the kitchen doorway. "Miss Dalton said she had a very hard time choosing because all the plays were good." Her mom was already going through the mail on the counter. "But mine was the best," Tara added softly.

Over the weekend Tara watched Melanie print out eight copies of the play. The clatter of the printer drowned out Rhett banging his Yo-Yo on the wall as he tried to Walk the Dog.

While the pages rolled out of the printer in long perforated sheets, the play unfolded in Tara's mind. In living color, she imagined Lizzie, clutching her baby, crashing through the snowy woods as she tried to stay ahead of the slave catchers.

Tara's heart beat faster as she pictured the terrified slave woman peering over her shoulder. Lizzie would have gasped as the slave catchers broke through the underbrush behind her. Racing with her baby through the bleak woods, Lizzie would know her only chance was to get across the frozen river to freedom.

Tara almost felt the slave's terror as she slipped down the banks of the river, only to find the ice was breaking up. Chunks as big as boats floated in the thawed part of the river.

Could she run across, from one ice floe to another, without dropping her baby? She looked around. The two slave catchers were pounding down the path behind her. It was now or never. She'd have to risk it—her only chance to get across the river alive.

"Here're your copies. Eight, right?"

Tara blinked, dazed, as she was yanked back through history abruptly. "Um, yes, eight copies should do it."

After mentally rehearsing each scene all weekend, she gave Miss Dalton the copies Monday morning. Tara'd thought about the casting a lot and knew who should play all the major characters. It was essential to give the parts of Lizzie, Mandy, Elijah, and John Fairfield to the right people.

Tara sniffed at the rose on her teacher's desk. "Even if I won't be acting in my play, can I watch the tryouts?" she asked.

Miss Dalton balanced on the corner of her desk. "I'm not sure that would be the best idea. Tryouts are tense for some kids, and having their friends in the audience might make it worse."

"Oh." Tara flipped through a copy of the play. "Well, if you want, I could make a list of all the characters we'll need. I have some suggestions of who'd be best for each part."

"I'd appreciate your making that list of characters. You can read it to the class after I remind everyone of the tryouts." She handed Tara a blank piece of paper. "But I think the tryouts should be open to anyone who's interested. Mr. Winsor always watches with me, and he'll help make the final choices."

Tara nodded. She guessed she didn't want to watch the tryouts anyway, if the principal was going to be there. Mr. Winsor *growled*—all the time—even when he wasn't mad.

Tara raced to school early Tuesday morning to see who'd been chosen for her play. Miss Dalton had prom-

·ised to post the cast list before going home the night before.

Inside the school, Tara held her breath and tiptoed past the principal's office. Mr. Winsor pounced on kids whenever he found them indoors before school hours.

She peered around the corner and spotted Mr. Winsor strutting down the hall in the opposite direction. Tara waited till he disappeared, then slithered around the corner and sped to her classroom. Sure enough, posted on the door, was a big sign:

CONGRATULATIONS TO THE CAST OF
SIXTH GRADE DRAMA NIGHT!
appearing in
"Smuggled to Safety"
by Tara Brown

Tara drew in a deep breath and let it out slowly. If it was this exciting to see her name printed on a cardboard sign, she knew she'd faint reading it on a program. She scanned the list quickly.

"Elijah—Richard Weston." She groaned softly. Richard *was* a good actor, but he clowned around so much.

"John Fairfield—Peter Griffith. Good," Tara mumbled. "Young slave girl—Vicki Jacobs." Tara frowned, but guessed that might work out after all. Vicki was a quiet, jumpy girl, but the slave girl didn't have a speaking part. She just had to act nervous, which Vicki did all the time.

Tara skimmed the rest of the list hurriedly, not wanting Mr. Winsor to catch her. "Oliver Steel and Jake Carter—slave catchers. Beverly Roth, Lizzie. Ugh! Not her," she muttered. "Let's see, Sherman Tool—director. Tara Brown—assistant. Karin Allen—chairman, scenery committee. Amber McCubbin—intermission entertainment."

Footsteps echoing from around the corner made Tara jump. Silently, she sneaked into her dark classroom and hung up her coat, thinking about the tryouts. Mostly, she was happy with the cast. She just hoped Richard would be serious long enough to learn his part. Suddenly, in the shadowy room, Tara grinned. One thing would be fun. She couldn't wait to see Beverly's waist-length blond hair stuffed up under a curly black wig.

By two o'clock when Miss Dalton announced rehearsal time, Tara's insides were like overwound springs. At last—the moment she'd been waiting for. She'd get to see her play come alive.

"I'll help, Miss Dalton." Tara jumped up, pushing aside desks to make room to practice. She guessed they wouldn't use the auditorium stage until later.

In spite of the confusion, five minutes later the actors were ready to rehearse. Peter, who played Fairfield, was gone to a dental appointment, so they would work on the second scene first. Karin's committee left for the art room to start on the scenery.

Miss Dalton smiled at Sherman. "Why don't you come up front, Mr. Director, and explain what you'd like your cast members to do."

Pushing his blurry glasses back up on his nose, Sherman shuffled to the blackboard. "Well, why don't we just sit and read through it first? Then maybe, um, we'll act some of it out."

Tara was on her feet instantly. "Since everyone read through the play last night for tryouts, they should get used to speaking on their feet."

Sherman blinked his owl eyes. "I guess that makes sense. Um, let's see. I want the mother, Lizzie, plus the two slave catchers, to come up front first."

Tara inched forward to the edge of her seat, her skin prickling. Lizzie's escape was a tense scene. She knew exactly how it should be played to be the most dramatic.

Miss Dalton stopped beside her. "Tara, could you take this note to Karin in the art room for me?" she asked, laying a paper on her desk. "It's about requesting paint for the horse and wagon and trees in the woods. I need her to check the colors."

"Now?"

"Yes, please."

Tara sighed, grabbed the list, and dashed out the door. She hated to miss a minute of rehearsal, but maybe running errands was part of her assistant's job.

She raced down the hall, but Karin wasn't in the art room. Janet said she'd gone to borrow some hammers and saws from the janitor. Tara tore down to the basement storage room, but it was locked. Exasperated, she took the narrow stairs two at a time.

Tara checked in the principal's office, but the secretary hadn't seen Karin all day. However, she knew the janitor was working in the gym, if Tara wanted to check there.

Fuming under her breath, Tara marched down the hall in the opposite direction. At this rate she'd miss the entire rehearsal! In the gym she spotted the janitor, high on a ladder changing bulbs protected by wire cages.

"Mr. Gordon?" Tara called, fidgeting. "Have you seen Karin Allen?"

The janitor snapped the wire cage shut. "A minute ago. You just missed her. She borrowed my hammer and saw."

"Thanks." Tara trotted back to the art room, where she found Karin at last. She was explaining how to cut pieces of plywood for the wagon wheels, then paint on the spokes.

"Finally." Tara thrust the note at Karin. "You're supposed to check this list of paint and then requisition it."

Karin glanced at the list, then handed it back to Tara. "Miss Dalton forgot yellow." Picking up a saw, she added, "Give that to the office secretary. She requisitions the supplies."

"*Me?*" Tara's voice rose above the noise of hammers and saws. "I can't do everything! I'm supposed to be helping Sherman direct the rehearsal right now."

Karin raised one eyebrow. "Well, excuse me."

Tara gulped at Karin's sarcastic look. She hadn't meant to snap at her. "Sorry. I'll drop off the list on my way back to the room." Turning, she retraced her steps to the office and left the paint list.

They were already rehearsing the last half of the scene when she got back to the classroom. Beverly, as the terrified slave mother, pretended to hold a baby as she peered around an imaginary tree trunk.

" 'Lord, help! Lord, save me!' " Staring at her script, she pretended to grip the baby in her arms. " 'May God help me, I won't let them get you!' " She tiptoed across the room.

Sherman pointed to the door at the back. "Now, remember, you'll be offstage for this part."

Puzzled, Tara watched Beverly prance to the back of the room. What was going on? Lizzie still had to cross the river on frozen chunks of ice—it wasn't time for her exit yet.

Beverly's absurd southern accent floated to the front of the room. " 'Oh, mercy! Where's the boat tha' takes people over?' " She gasped and clutched her throat. " 'The boats has stopped runnin'!' "

Sherman nodded. "Now, here's where someone will make splashing sound effects, while Beverly—er, Lizzie—screams and yells a little."

Tara tapped her script with her fingernail. "This isn't right," she muttered. All that action wasn't supposed to happen offstage.

Eeeeks! and *help-helps!* and *oh-no's!* punctuated the air. Sherman had his eyes closed, listening. He nodded slowly. "That should work out fine, I think."

"Oh no, it won't!" Tara strode to the front of the room. "This is the most exciting part of the second scene! You can't have her cross the dangerous river offstage. The audience has to see this part."

Sherman pointed to the wood floor and shrugged. "We can't make a river for her to cross, complete with chunks of ice."

"We have to," Tara insisted. "Otherwise there won't be anything for the audience to watch."

"Yes, there will. I thought we'd show the slave catchers getting closer and closer as they chase Lizzie."

Gritting her teeth, Tara glanced at their teacher. She wished Miss Dalton would speak up, but she was absorbed in grading papers.

Tara scratched her head. "We could make a river out of blue painted cardboard or something. Big flat rocks would make good ice floes. Beverly could walk across the river on them."

"I never thought of that." Sherman removed his spotty glasses, wiped them with his shirttail, and slid them back on. "Okay, Beverly, come back up here and pretend you're going across a frozen river."

Sitting back down, Tara was relieved Sherman had listened. She'd imagined this dramatic scene so many times, and it had to be done right.

For the rest of the rehearsal, Tara stayed at her desk, following along in her script with a red pencil. Even with Beverly having to pretend the floor was a river, the scene came alive.

Tara smiled to herself. If the scene was gripping now, just wait till the actors wore their costumes and black wigs, performing on the auditorium stage with the lights turned low.

In her mind, Tara could already hear the thunderous applause.

4

Ski Masks
and Greasepaint

Tara straightened her shoulders, smiled into the bathroom mirror, and began, "Brave Union men and women jeopardized their own safety—" Her squeaky voice cracked. Frowning, Tara cleared her throat. "Uh, hem." Holding her note cards closer, she lowered her voice an octave.

"Brave Union men and women jeopardized their own safety," she growled, "to help slaves escape to freedom by way of the Underground Railroad. Estimates of the number of slaves who escaped range from 25,000 to 100,000. This was only a tiny fraction of the total slave population, which was about four million in 1860. John Fairfield—"

"Who's in there?" Melanie yelled. "Sounds like Dracula."

Tara flung open the door. "I'm practicing my play introduction. I'm trying to sound serious, but my voice keeps squeaking."

Melanie stepped in front of Tara and peered at her braces. "I thought so," she murmured, reaching for the dental floss. She sawed back and forth between her teeth, spraying spit all over the mirror. "Why do you need an introduction, anyway?"

"To set a serious mood. Otherwise Richard's clowning or Amber's tap dance will wreck the atmosphere."

"Who's giving the introduction?"

"Me, of course. I know exactly the tone I want to set. Hey, what if I dressed in 1850s clothes?" Tara tried to imagine her straight brown hair swirled up high on her head.

"It won't matter what you look like. Nobody will listen anyway. While you're speaking, all the parents will talk to each other or take little kids to the bathroom before the play starts." She rinsed her retainer under the faucet.

"Oh. Well, I'll just have to do something to get their attention." Tara tapped her cards on the counter. "I know! I'll give the introduction in total darkness, except for one spotlight on me. Then it will be too dark for people to talk or move around." Nodding, she started over from the beginning.

* * *

The next afternoon the first scene actors grouped at the front of the room. This time they would rehearse where the slave catchers captured part of the family John Fairfield was smuggling away. Played just right, Tara felt it would leave the audience on the edge of their seats.

Miss Dalton nodded at Sherman. "Go ahead and begin. I'll be right back after I check on something in the art room."

Tara eagerly turned in her script to Scene One. In the first part Fairfield would hide the fugitive slaves in his wagon and start through the woods. Oliver Steel, one of the slave catchers, crouched behind an imaginary tree. Richard strolled by him, casually dropping a paper sack at Oliver's feet, then took his position next to Vicki.

Puzzled, Oliver opened the sack, then jerked and dropped it to the floor. "Hey!" he yelled as Limburger scurried out. "Get that mouse!"

Richard doubled over, hooting and slapping his leg. Sherman dove for the mouse and collided with Oliver. Racing around the teacher's desk, Tara spotted Limburger scurrying behind the bean-bag chair in the corner.

"There he is," she yelled, pointing. "Somebody get him!"

"I will, I will," Richard called, still holding his shaking sides. In one quick sweep, he scooped up the quivering mouse and deposited him in the science maze.

The excitement over, Tara turned on Richard angrily. "We're never going to get anything done if you don't knock it off!"

"Oh, cool it," Richard said, blowing a bubble and popping it. A thin layer of purple gum covered his nose, mouth, and chin.

Tara gritted her teeth. Most of the time she really liked Richard. He livened up her boring spelling and music classes, but at this rate he would ruin her play.

"Sherman?" She turned to the director. "Tell him to stop messing around."

Nodding, he mumbled, "We do need to get back to work."

Just then Miss Dalton returned, and with an elaborate bow, Richard went back to his place.

"Action!"

Richard, Vicki, and Beverly huddled together under a table that was to serve as a wagon during rehearsal.

Peter, as John Fairfield, sat on top and flapped imaginary reins. " 'Stay down, back there. The woods are full of bounty hunters and slave catchers. If we run into one—' "

" 'Oh, surely, Suh, you won't tell anyone we ah heah!' " Richard said, hand over his heart.

" 'Never! You've earned your liberty!' " Peter declared. " 'And you shall have it.' "

" 'The Lord bless you.' "

" 'It's your folks up North that's paying your way.' "

" 'Jus' the same, I sho' do thank ye. Ma whole fambly thanks ye.' "

Exasperated, Tara cleared her throat and tapped Sherman on the back. He glanced over his shoulder. "You want something?"

"Richard's slave dialect stinks. I can barely understand what he's saying, and *I* wrote the words." She shook her head. "No one in the audience will understand him either."

"He is laying it on kind of thick." Sherman raised his voice. "Richard, you're talking so weird we can't tell what you're saying."

"Sorry, massah," Richard drawled, bowing low. "Hey, what about our costumes? What did slaves wear, anyway?"

"Old ragged clothes should be okay." Sherman polished his smeared glasses. "We can rip and tear them some to look authentic."

"He still won't look like a slave," Oliver said. Tara agreed, studying Richard's light skin and freckles. Oliver snapped his fingers. "I know!"

He ran to the row of hooks where the winter coats hung. From a bulging pocket he pulled a black knit ski mask. He jammed it down over his head, leaving only his eyes and mouth showing. "How about this?"

Tara rolled her eyes. He couldn't be serious.

But Sherman nodded. "That looks okay. At least his face will be the right color. Could you round up more ski masks for the rest of the slaves?"

"No, he won't!" Tara marched down the aisle. The image of her perfect play was fading faster each minute. "I didn't write a Christmas play. With the actors in ski masks, the audience would start singing 'Jingle Bells'!"

For support, Tara turned to Miss Dalton, who simply smiled and shrugged. Tara knew Miss Dalton preferred that the kids settle their own differences. She called it a "learning experience for life." She only played referee if it got too loud or someone got punched.

Tara turned back to Sherman, hands firmly on her hips. "Stocking caps won't do."

"Got any better ideas?"

"Real actors use greasepaint." Tara tried to remember what stuff Rhett had used on his face at Halloween to look like a vampire bat. "I'll get some."

Beverly's piercing voice came from under the table. "I'm not going to wear any greasepaint on *my* face. It clogs the pores and gives you permanent blackheads. I won't get zits just for some dumb play."

Clenching her teeth, Tara said, "If you don't wear make-up, Lizzie won't look right."

"She only has to be dark tan. I'll use a sun lamp." Beverly flipped her long mane over her shoulder.

Tara chewed her lip thoughtfully. Actually, maybe

a dark tan would be okay. Still, did Beverly have to argue about *everything*?

Peter Griffith looked up from coloring his fingernails with glow-in-the-dark markers. "When do the slave catchers jump out and shoot me? Isn't that pretty soon?"

"Right." Sherman nodded. "Turn to page thirteen in your scripts. Get in place for when John Fairfield gets wounded and Elijah and Mandy are captured."

Oliver and Jake, as the cruel slave catchers, drifted to one side of the room. The fugitive slaves hid under the table on the other side.

"Action." Sherman pointed to Oliver and Jake.

"I hate to interrupt," Miss Dalton said. "I just wanted to point out that the stage curtain will only extend to the edges of the chalkboard. The actors can't be spread clear across the room because the stage won't be that big."

Sherman motioned the boys to move in closer together. "How's that?"

"Fine. The curtain will stretch that far."

Tara hurried to Miss Dalton's desk. "I don't understand. Won't we be doing the play in the auditorium?"

Miss Dalton shook her head. "No, I thought you knew. We've always held Drama Night in here. Mr. Winsor only allows full school productions to be held in the auditorium—like the band or vocal concerts."

Tara couldn't believe it. No auditorium? Her stomach began to churn. She burped, tasting her taco chips from lunch.

Two years ago, when Melanie was in sixth grade, Tara had been sick and missed Drama Night. She'd always assumed the play was performed in the auditorium, with a real stage, colored spotlights, and ushers with programs. Performing in the classroom, behind a makeshift stage, would look so babyish. Her parents would never be impressed by *that*.

Tara tapped the green fish paperweight on Miss Dalton's desk. "Um, could you at least ask Mr. Winsor if we could use the auditorium?"

"The chances wouldn't be very good, Tara. Mr. Winsor rarely bends his rules, even for a good reason. Believe me, on other occasions I've tried."

"But my play would look so much better on a real stage, don't you think?"

"It probably would look more professional." Miss Dalton studied Tara's face for a moment, then pushed back her chair. "You're right—it can't hurt to ask. If he says no, we won't have lost anything, will we?"

Tara beamed. "Thanks for asking."

"Don't get your hopes up," Miss Dalton warned. "Just keep your fingers crossed that I catch him in a good mood." She raised her voice. "I have an errand to run. Finish this scene quietly, then take your seats."

"Take them where?" Richard asked. He slapped

Oliver on the back and laughed, his gum falling to the floor.

"Come on, guys, let's finish the last page." Sherman pointed to Oliver. "Start right where you jump out from behind the trees and shoot Fairfield."

The rehearsal went on, but Tara's mind was on Miss Dalton. If only she could talk their touchy principal into letting them use the auditorium. Her play deserved a dignified setting. And that would be impossible, if performed behind a mildewed curtain strung across the classroom.

Ten minutes later Miss Dalton returned and stopped at Tara's desk. "It took some persuading, but we can use the auditorium after all," her teacher announced with a grin. "I should have asked before."

"Great!" Tara jumped, startling the mice in the nearby cage.

Miss Dalton shook Tara's hand as if closing an important deal. "We do have to strictly follow certain rules, though, about use of the lights and cleaning up afterwards."

"I'll take care of all that," Tara promised. Even if she had to vacuum the entire auditorium by herself after the play, it would be worth it.

"Then I'll leave it in your capable hands." Miss Dalton squeezed her shoulder, then went back to her desk.

Tara knelt down with her face close to the mice cage. "It may be the whole class's Drama Night," she whispered to Limburger, "but it's still *my* first play. If I have anything to say, it's going to be perfect."

☙ 5 ❧

Read All About It

Peter Griffith strolled to the front of the room, holding a colorful piece of paper in his hand. "Attention, you-all," he drawled.

"What do you have there?" Miss Dalton asked.

"My dad said he'd make a real program for our play," Peter said proudly. "This is just a rough sketch of it."

Tara leaned forward eagerly, remembering Peter's father was a commercial artist. She'd planned to have mimeographed programs to hand out at the auditorium doors, but certainly nothing designed by a professional. Maybe her class was taking the play more seriously than she'd thought.

Beverly wrapped her long hair around her head like a turban. "Well, do we get to see it?"

"Sure. Of course, this is just a sketch, not the finished program." Peter went slowly up and down the aisles. "It lists the characters inside, and even tells a little about slaves and slave smuggling."

Tara snapped to attention. "I was going to tell about slave smuggling in my introduction," she interrupted.

"What introduction?" Beverly yawned delicately.

Tara turned to Miss Dalton. "I'll be giving some background that leads up to John Fairfield helping the slaves to escape."

Peter pointed to a paragraph inside the program. "Dad gave some background right here. Why do you have to give an introduction on stage?"

"Look, she wrote the play," Amber said. "Let her give an introduction if she wants to."

Miss Dalton placed her hand on Peter's shoulder. "Perhaps we can leave the general information about slave smuggling in the program," she said. "Then Tara could tell how the Underground Railroad got started and where it was operated. How about that?"

Tara took the program Miss Dalton held out. "I guess that's okay." She studied the pale blue cover, with Civil War hats and crossed bayonets sketched at the top. "These drawings look real, but—"

"—but what?" Peter demanded.

"Army hats and swords don't have anything to do with the scenes in my play." Tara licked her lips. "I'll

59

loan you my library copy of *The Illustrated History of the Civil War* before your dad does the final sketch. Maybe he could copy a picture of fugitive slaves for the cover."

Richard blew a bubble and it popped. "Pick, pick, pick."

"I'm not being picky," Tara protested. "I just want everything to be as perfect as possible."

Peter looked at the sketch again, then shoved the paper onto the floor. "Why don't you make the program yourself, Miss Perfect?"

Tara jerked back as if she'd been slapped. "I didn't mean—I was only trying to help," she stammered. But Peter had already gone back to his desk.

Tara slumped down in her seat, noticing Beverly's smirk and Miss Dalton's puckered forehead. She bent to pick up the program, stewing inwardly. Why was Peter so touchy all of a sudden? Tara only wanted this play to be the best any sixth grade had ever performed. It would make them *all* look good, not just her.

Hiding behind her open science book, she studied the program more closely. Five minutes later, she was actually glad to be doing the program herself after all.

For one thing, in Peter's program the cast was merely listed by name. Tara shook her head; it wasn't enough. Each character needed a short sentence explaining who he was, and where he fit into the play.

And that cover. Besides the drawings being wrong,

the letter sizes were off. The title of the play was in huge letters, but her own name was smaller than Sherman's, and he was only the director.

Tara slipped the program into her desk, then took it home at the end of the day to study over the weekend. By Saturday afternoon, she had several ideas and dragged Melanie away from her school books to help with her cover design.

Tara pointed to a drawing of a slave, partly covered with hay, hidden in the back of a wagon. "Could you copy this picture onto the cover?" she asked. "It only has to be in black and white. We'll run them off on the copy machine in Mr. Winsor's office."

Melanie studied the sketch. "I guess so. How big do you want it?"

"I figure it should fill the middle of the page." Tara penciled a light circle on the paper. "I'll put the title and my name at the top, and Sherman's name on the bottom."

While Melanie drew at the table, Tara worked on the one-line character descriptions for the inside. By the time she'd done the descriptions of Lizzie, Mandy, Elijah, John Fairfield, and the slave catchers, Melanie was finished.

"Here. How's this?" She handed Tara a delicate ink drawing.

"All right! It's super!"

After Melanie left, Tara sat staring at the drawing. It was full of tension and suspense, so much better than the Civil War hats. She *did* wish Peter hadn't been so sensitive about it, though. When he'd said his program was just a rough sketch, she honestly thought he'd want suggestions.

It took Tara most of Sunday afternoon to type up the inside of the program. Melanie set up the computer for her before leaving for the library. Although Melanie'd had typing at school, Tara used her dad's hunt and peck system. Slow, but it worked.

Monday morning Tara cornered Miss Dalton at the back of the room. "I worked on the program over the weekend. What do you think?" she whispered. She didn't want Peter to see it yet. After a while maybe he'd forget all about it and not be mad.

"This sketch is dramatic—right in keeping with the mood of your play." Miss Dalton slipped the program back into its large manila envelope. "I'll get copies run off soon."

"Thanks." Tara hesitated. "You know, I wasn't making fun of Peter's program last week." Her heart thudded under her sweater and the back of her neck got sweaty.

"I know." With long cool fingers, Miss Dalton smoothed Tara's hair back over her shoulder. "Sometimes words don't come out the way we mean them."

"Usually Peter's not so touchy."

Miss Dalton leaned her head to one side. "Maybe he thought you were saying his dad wasn't too great as an artist. You suppose?"

"Maybe." Tara felt kind of sick. She hadn't thought of that. Sighing, she turned to look at Peter, then shuffled to her desk, stopping beside him on the way. "Hi. Could I ask you something?"

Peter continued to draw lightning bolts on his notebook cover. "What?"

"Um, I wondered if you knew how to make the woods in the play look more real?"

"How would I know?"

Tara shuffled her feet back and forth. "You could ask your dad for some ideas."

Peter looked skeptical. "You'd want to hear his ideas?"

"Sure, he's a professional artist, isn't he?" Tara swallowed and kept a smile pasted on her face.

"I guess I could ask. He could probably think of dozens of ideas."

"Great! That would really help the scenery committee. Well, see you." Moving on, Tara let out the breath she'd been holding.

That afternoon's rehearsal time was spent on Scene Two, where Lizzie escaped over the frozen river. Beverly, clutching a doll someone had donated, spotted the slave catchers and ran to the river bank. Once there, however, she pranced across daintily on tiptoes, swaying wildly back and forth.

"Cut! Cut!" Sherman waved his script. "What are you doing, Beverly?"

"Pretending I have my costume on. Hoop skirts are hard to run in, and they swing back and forth."

"Hoop skirts?" Tara snorted aloud. "Lizzie was a slave. Only the rich ladies on the plantations wore hoop skirts. You'll wear a dark shirt or dress."

"Oh, no, I won't." Beverly shook the doll till its plastic eyes rattled. "I'll wear the dumb curly wig, but I'm not wearing some ugly dress too."

"But you can't wear a hoop skirt. It won't look right. Slaves didn't wear fancy clothes." Tara held up the illustration in her library book. "See?"

"Who cares what's in that stupid book?" Beverly plopped down in the middle of the stage. "If I can't wear a hoop skirt, I won't be in the play."

Tara clenched her fists and turned to Miss Dalton. However, her teacher looked totally unconcerned. Scowling, Tara wished *she* were the teacher—she'd smack Beverly.

She turned back to Sherman who shrugged and looked at his shoes. "There really isn't time for someone else to learn Beverly's part."

Beverly smirked from her position on the floor.

Tara glared at Beverly. "I guess a hoop skirt wouldn't look so bad," she grudgingly agreed.

"Good." Beverly smiled sweetly at Sherman. "Shall we take it from the top?"

Amber leaned over, sticking her tongue out behind her hand. "That Beverly's such a dipstick."

"That's for sure."

Tara leaned back. A slave in a hoop skirt *would* look dumb. In the end, though, she figured it wouldn't matter. If the tap dancer didn't steal the show, a slave in a hoop skirt would hardly be noticed.

❧ 6 ❧

Jinxed

Richard flung candy wrappers, crumpled quizzes, and dried-up wads of chewing gum out of his desk. The garbage piled up around him on the floor until his desk was empty.

"I *told* you it's not here." Richard twirled an imaginary mustache. "A thief is on the loose!"

Sherman sorted through the junk on the floor. "If you didn't take the script home, you probably lost it."

Tara's breath hissed through her teeth. One more delay! She could easily run off another copy at home, but she'd spent a lot of time penciling in special directions on each individual script.

Miss Dalton stopped at his desk. "Why don't you borrow Tara's script, then look for your own later. There's not much rehearsal time left."

Tara passed her script to Richard. "Here."

Richard flipped a stick of gum through the air. "Thanks," he said as the bubblegum hit Tara on the nose.

Tara stuck the gum in her pocket as the cast shuffled into position. She hated giving up her script. Since no one had been assigned the job of prompter, she'd been doing it. If she concentrated real hard, though, maybe she could remember most of the lines.

"Richard, pretend like you're hidden in the wagon," Sherman directed. "When you hear the slave catcher's gun, jump from the wagon and run across the stage toward those trees."

Richard crouched down in the make-believe wagon. Tara rubbed the goose bumps on her arms. She *loved* this part.

"Action!"

Oliver and Jake pointed their cap guns in the air, grinning at the loud pops they made. On cue Beverly screamed. Tara sighed. Beverly's long, drawn-out wail sounded like someone who had fallen off the Empire State Building, and was screaming in agony all the way to the ground.

Richard popped up in pretended shock. At her second scream, he took off for the woods. He never reached the other side.

Halfway across the "stage," he threw up his hands,

then flipped over on his back. His head smacked the wooden floor with a loud *thunk*.

This time Beverly screamed for real, while Sherman, Tara, and Miss Dalton rushed to Richard. Sherman helped him sit up. "Hey! You okay?"

"Yeah, sure," Richard snapped, rubbing the back of his head. "Feels great to bounce your head off the floor."

Tara noticed a dark stain on the back of Richard's shirt, then touched the floor. It was wet. "Looks like someone spilled some water here," she said, wiping it up with a paper towel.

Amber met her at the wastebasket. "What happened up there?" she asked. "I was in the restroom."

"Richard slipped in a puddle of water and cracked his head." Tara frowned. "He says he's okay."

"No sweat. Accidents happen."

"True. If it *was* an accident."

"What do you mean?"

"Well, first Richard's script is missing. Then he 'accidentally' slips in a pool of water conveniently spilled where he'd have to run through it."

"You mean on purpose?" Amber watched Miss Dalton check through Richard's hair for signs of a cut. "Nobody'd want to hurt Richard."

"Except—maybe someone's jealous he got the lead part?"

Amber shook her head. "I doubt it. You know how Richard messes around. This is the kind of dumb thing he'd do just to show off." She *tap-tapped* off down the aisle, humming "Way Down upon the Suwannee River."

Scratching her head, Tara decided Amber was probably right. Richard *did* act like a nut. Usually he was a scream to watch, but not during rehearsals. Gritting her teeth, Tara saw that half the practice time was over already.

Karin Allen came back from the art room just then and pushed through the group around Richard. "Miss Dalton? We finished the wagon, then started on the tree pattern Peter's dad gave us. But no way can we make a frozen river. Also, where are we going to find enough cotton for everyone to hide under?"

"I think Tara had an idea about the frozen river," Miss Dalton said.

Tara nodded, explaining to Karin about the blue construction paper river, dotted with foil-covered rocks for ice chunks.

"Okay, that should work. Now, what about cotton for the wagon?"

Tara sighed. Did she have to think of *everything*? "Well, how about the insides of an old couch or mattress? The stuffing would look like cotton."

Karin frowned. "You know anybody who wants to donate a bed we can shred?"

"No, I don't! *You're* the chairman of the scenery committee."

Miss Dalton turned and put a hand on both their shoulders. "I know someone trying to dispose of an old couch."

"Who?" Tara asked.

"My landlady. She's going to take it to the dump, I think."

"Do you think she'd let us have it?"

"I don't know that we'd need the whole thing, but I'm sure she'd give us the loose cushions. I'll bring them to school."

Tara nodded. "We can pull out the stuffing here. Thanks, Miss Dalton."

The next afternoon before rehearsal Tara watched in amazement as Beverly modeled her homemade costume. She pranced back and forth across the stage to show Sherman the hoop skirt she'd constructed. Richard's shrieks and howls drowned out Beverly's words.

"Where did you get *that* contraption?" Richard asked between gasps. "You look like a walking mushroom."

"Don't be unkind, Richard," Miss Dalton said. "That's a very interesting skirt shape, Beverly."

"Thank you," Beverly said, sticking out her tongue at Richard. She lifted the edges of the skirt, showing her jeans underneath. "I took the cloth off our old beach umbrella and sewed the spokes to the underside of this skirt." Two yardsticks, attached to the bottom ends of the spokes, kept the umbrella spokes pushed out. Beverly's legs straddled the crossed yardsticks.

Dropping the material, Beverly twirled around. The skirt stuck out horizontally from her waist, in a definite umbrella shape, then dropped straight to the floor. It was the weirdest thing Tara'd ever seen.

Sherman polished his cloudy glasses, put them back on, and stared again at Beverly's umbrella dress. Shrugging, he finally called, "Places, everybody."

The Scene Two actors moved up front, and the others shuffled to the back of the room to memorize lines. Beverly swayed back and forth, clutching Lizzie's baby.

"Page four." Sherman flipped open his script. "This part needs more work. Richard, Elijah has to sound braver here, not totally scared out of his wits. Beverly, when Lizzie and Elijah whisper about their plans for when they reach Canada, you'll have to whisper louder. No one past the front row can hear you."

Surprised, Tara nodded in agreement. Sherman was finally getting the hang of directing.

"Action!"

The scene went smoothly as Elijah tried to reassure Lizzie about their dangerous situation. Vicki Jacobs, as the slave girl, pretended to hush the crying baby. Lizzie was almost hysterical, and Elijah wiped her teary eyes. At the end of the scene Elijah was to gently kiss his wife.

Richard leaned near Beverly, smiled tenderly, and licked her cheek.

"Ugh!" Beverly jerked back and wiped her face. "Gross! My face is dripping!"

"Sorry." Richard smirked. "But cheer up. You can't get too wet when you're wearing an umbrella!"

The slave catchers bent double laughing, and the rehearsal fell apart. Tara pounded her fist on her knee. "I knew things were going too well," she muttered. Glancing toward the back of the room, she noticed Miss Dalton step out the door.

Beverly suddenly whirled, grabbed the doll from Vicki, and slugged Richard in the stomach with it. "I've had it," she cried. "This is *it*." Umbrella spokes swaying, she started down the aisle.

Tara jumped up and stood in her way. "Calm down, Beverly. Richard won't do it again."

"How do you know?" She whipped around to glare at Richard, sideswiping Tara with her long hair. "I quit. I'm telling Miss Dalton as soon as she comes back."

Blowing a huge purple bubble, Richard carefully took it from his mouth without popping it. He waved the sticky bubble under Beverly's nose. "Just having some fun."

"I don't care." Pouting, Beverly plopped down at

her desk, arms folded across her chest. Her spokes stuck out in front. "I won't be in this third-rate play."

"This is a *first*-rate play—just third-rate acting!" Tara sputtered. She pivoted on her heel and stomped to the back of the room where Amber was practicing her tap routine. "Beverly's such a *baby*," she snarled.

"Don't worry about her," Amber said. "She wouldn't miss being a star for anything. She only wants everybody to beg her to be in the play. Just watch." She nodded toward the door as Miss Dalton came in.

Sure enough, Beverly bounced up from her desk when she spotted Miss Dalton, as if nothing had happened. Sherman called out "Page six," and they went on.

Tara relaxed as they took their places again. The cap guns exploded twice, and Beverly, Vicki, and Richard jumped from the wagon. Beverly slipped behind a tree, and Richard dashed away, but Vicki moved with stiff, wooden movements.

First Vicki jerked her way over to where Beverly was hiding. Silently she handed the baby to its mother, then lurched after Richard.

Eyes wide, Tara watched closely. *Why* had Vicki Jacobs been chosen for that part? She was awful, moving like a robot in pain. This was her worst practice yet. If somebody didn't do something, Vicki would wreck the scene.

As Lizzie frantically wrapped her shawl around the

baby, Vicki shuffled across the stage, all hunched over. Tara studied Vicki's pinched face. It was a funny clay color. Maybe she wasn't a terrible actress after all. Maybe she was sick instead.

"Vicki," Tara interrupted, "do you feel all right?"

Vicki turned with a jerk and blinked rapidly. "Yes. Yes, of course." She gulped. "Why?"

"You're walking so funny. I thought maybe you had a stomach ache."

Blushing poppy red, Vicki's cheek twitched. Then, to Tara's horror, she burst into tears and ran from the room.

7

The Latest Fashion

Stunned, Tara watched Vicki disappear through the door, then shrank back as Karin charged down the aisle straight toward her. Hands on hips, Karin stopped with her face six inches from Tara's. "I hope you're satisfied now!"

"What did I do?" Tara demanded, feeling heat creep up her neck to her cheeks.

Karin's eyes flashed. "You think you're so hot. Just because the class is doing your play, you think it has to be so wonderful. But you had no right to say Vicki was terrible."

"I never said that!"

"Right in the middle of the scene you called her a sick-looking actress."

"Well, she *was* walking pretty weird." Tara wished

the other kids would stop staring at them. "I didn't mean to hurt her feelings." Tara shuffled her feet nervously as Miss Dalton came up the aisle.

"Can I help with something here?" she mumbled around the straight pins in her mouth. She held a slave's black shirt with a half-sewn-on patch.

Karin turned her back on Tara. "Can I go to the restroom? Vicki needed some help with something."

Miss Dalton looked from Karin to Tara, but merely nodded. When Karin left, Miss Dalton sat on the edge of Tara's desk and continued sewing on the patch. "Want to talk about it?"

Tara waited until the others drifted away. "Vicki was walking all hunched over during the rehearsal and I asked her if she was sick or something."

"Mmmm. I gather she wasn't?"

"Karin said she was just nervous in front of everybody."

"I see. That was probably it." Miss Dalton laid the slave shirt in her lap, then put her arm around Tara's shoulders. "I wouldn't worry too much. Vicki may have been embarrassed, but I'm sure when she thinks about it, she'll be pleased that you were concerned about her. Your heart was in the right place." She squeezed Tara's arm, then slid off her desk. "Would you like me to talk to her?"

Tara nodded, hoping Miss Dalton was right. Gathering her books to take home, Tara wished for a minute that Miss Dalton was her real mother. She was so easy to talk to. Tara bet Miss Dalton would love all her kids exactly the same too, even if they weren't perfect.

Tara arrived at school the next morning before Amber, and waited for her by the corner of the building. The final buzzer sounded, but she still hadn't shown up. Tara hurried inside, hoping Amber was just late again and not sick.

Five minutes later, while Miss Dalton was taking roll, the door at the front of the classroom flew open. "*Ta-da!*" Amber called out, then sailed into the room.

Tara couldn't believe her eyes. Amber flounced back and forth in front of the room. From the waist down, over her jeans, she wore what looked like hoops for an invisible skirt.

Three different sized hoops were suspended from ropes tied to Amber's belt. Tara stared closely. Just below her waist hung a small metal hoop—it looked like a bike tire rim. About a foot below that, hanging from more ropes, was a larger bike rim. And below that, an orange hula hoop was suspended, swinging slightly as Amber walked.

She stopped, fanning herself with a paper fan. "Well, what do you-*all* think?"

Richard groaned. "I'm almost afraid to ask. What is it?"

"What do you mean, what is it? It's hoops for Beverly's skirt. Now she won't look like a walking umbrella."

Miss Dalton circled Amber slowly, gazing at the maze of hoops and ropes. "Genius. Pure genius."

Amber smirked at Richard. "I put this together last night from junk in the garage. Mom gave me this hula hoop—it was hers when she was a kid."

Beverly frowned. "Won't that thing take all day to put on?"

"Nope." Amber grinned. "Watch."

She unbuckled the heavy leather belt the hoops were anchored to. Keeping the ropes untangled, she stepped out of the center of the hoops. "*Voila!*"

While Richard whistled, Tara clapped. Amber was nuts, but this crazy idea looked as if it might work. Since Beverly insisted on wearing a hoop skirt, this would make it more authentic. Still laughing, Tara grabbed her English and spelling books and headed for Miss Button's class.

As Tara reached the door, Amber grabbed her arm. "Tara! Listen!"

"I loved those hoops!" Tara said. "How did you ever—"

"Shh!" Amber glanced over her shoulders. "I found out something awful this morning. It's about Miss Dalton."

Tara froze at Amber's tone of voice. "What is it?"

"You know my dad's on the school board. I heard him and Mom talking before breakfast."

Tara glanced up and saw Miss Dalton coming their way. She elbowed Amber in the ribs and raised her voice. *"How did you think of that hoop idea?"*

Amber's mouth fell open. "Didn't you hear what I said?"

"Let's go, girls." Miss Dalton spoke briskly from behind Amber, who jumped. "I'm sure Miss Button wonders where you are, Tara."

"Sorry, I'm going." Heading out the door, Tara glanced back at Amber and nearly stumbled. She could swear Amber mouthed the words, *"Miss Dalton got fired!"*

The door swooshed shut before Amber's words hit her. Miss Dalton—fired? She *must* have misunderstood Amber. She never was any good at lip reading.

Next door in the other sixth grade, Tara couldn't keep her mind on the sonnets they were reading. Each minute seemed an hour long. She *had* to find out what Amber meant.

Later that morning at recess, Amber pulled Tara over to a corner of the playground. "The school board isn't exactly firing Miss Dalton," she explained. "They just aren't renewing her contract for next year."

"Isn't that the same thing?" Tara asked. She pulled her jacket collar close around her neck.

"Not really. Winchester Heights won't need as many teachers next year. Lots of kids have moved away, and some have transferred to that private school across town." Amber leaned against the chain-link fence. "The class sizes here are shrinking. This years' fifth grade classes will be scrunched into one sixth grade next year."

"But why get rid of Miss Dalton? She's a million times better teacher than old Miss Button!"

"That doesn't count. Of everybody who's left, Miss Dalton was hired last. The newest teacher gets fired first." The breeze whipped Amber's blond hair into her eyes. "She's good, though. She'll get a job somewhere else, easy."

Tara jammed her hands deep in her jeans pockets. "Even so, there's a million reasons why that's not fair."

For one, no other teacher in school put on a Drama Night. And no other teacher let her students have pen pals from France and Japan, or took her class snow camping. Miss Dalton even let them use the video camera for current events to tape their own news show. Miss Dalton made school fun, and now she was getting fired.

Tara shook the metal fence. "We've got to do something to stop this."

"We can't. Dad doesn't even know I overheard him."

"Good. We'll be able catch them by surprise then."

"Catch who?"

"The school board! We'll have to convince them they're making a mistake." The buzzer sounded and students surged toward the double doors.

Amber linked her arm through Tara's. "I feel bad too, but what can we do about it?" She lowered her voice as they joined the others. "Anyway, Dad would kill me if he knew I told, so keep quiet. It isn't worth getting in trouble for, especially since we can't change anything."

Tara didn't answer, but her mind was already whirling. The school board *couldn't* fire Miss Dalton. She was Winchester Heights' best teacher. Deep in thought, Tara trudged along beside the double rows of green lockers.

Several times during the rest of the day Tara caught herself staring at Miss Dalton. Tara couldn't imagine Winchester Heights without her. With a jolt, Tara realized how much she'd counted on Miss Dalton always being there, in case she wanted to drop in sometimes next year just to talk. She bet lots of kids felt the same way.

After school Tara was still preoccupied with Miss Dalton's crisis. "It's just not *fair*," she muttered, rummaging in her locker.

Suddenly Tara froze, her arm halfway into her locker as something clicked in her mind. *Now* she knew what this reminded her of: the slaves and the Underground Railroad.

When the slaves had had no rights—when they could

be bought and sold on a plantation owner's whim—Northerners had stepped in to fight that injustice, forming the Underground Railroad.

It was almost the same with Miss Dalton, Tara decided. She had no rights either! The school board, without a thought to fairness or who was the best teacher, could tell Miss Dalton she had to leave.

Tara squared her shoulders. Just like the Northerners had done, it was up to her to step in and fight *this* injustice. Somehow the school board's plans would have to be stopped.

"I'll start tonight," she vowed, kicking her locker shut. And idea began to form in her mind. "A letter to the editor of the *Chronicle* will be the first step. I'll explain to the whole town what a great teacher Miss Dalton is. Then the board wouldn't dare fire her!"

But, like the slave smugglers, Tara knew she'd have to move fast—before Miss Dalton's time ran out.

8

Chewing Gum
and Stuffing

That night Tara shut herself in her bedroom for two hours after supper and scribbled furiously. At eight-thirty she emerged, her fingers smudged with pencil lead. She stalked down the hall to the bathroom, clutching her letter to the editor.

"Melanie, are you in there?" Tara hit the door with her elbow. "I need a favor."

Melanie opened the door a crack and spoke through a foaming mouth. "Whuth?" She peeked down the hall, pulled Tara inside, then locked the door behind her.

"What's going on in here?" Tara poked among the tubes and tablets by the sink. "What are you doing with false teeth cleaners?"

Melanie spit out her foam. "I thought this Denture Stains-Away would clean my braces better, but this junk's so gritty." She rinsed and spit again, then pointed to a glass full of green bubbling water. "My retainer's soaking in there. I used one of those tablets that fizzes."

Tara shook her head. How could *anyone* be so fascinated with her own teeth? She held up her wrinkled paper. "Could you type this for me real fast?"

Melanie sighed. "Now what?"

"It's a letter to the editor. Amber's dad said Miss Dalton's getting fired."

"What? Why?" Melanie fished her retainer out of the green water. "She's the best teacher I ever had."

"I guess there's not enough kids to have two sixth grades next year. Amber said lots of them are going to that new private school."

"So you wrote a letter to protest Miss Dalton's getting fired?" Melanie looked proud of Tara. "Let me see."

She read quickly. "This is really good. But what about this?" Melanie pointed to the bold black signature at the bottom: Tara Brown, Representative of Miss Dalton's Sixth Grade. "Are you representing some committee?"

Tara thought for a minute, then snapped her fingers. "I will be tomorrow!" She grabbed the paper and changed her signature to read: Tara Brown, Chairperson of the Sixth Grade Save Miss Dalton Committee.

"I'll type it for you." Melanie replaced her dad's

denture cleaners. "You won't tell Dad I used his stuff, will you?"

"Cross my heart and hope to die, stick a needle in my eye," she promised. "While you type, can I use your phone? I want to call some kids in my class about joining this committee, but I need some privacy."

"I guess so, but you have to quit when I'm done with your letter."

"Deal." Tara scooted down the hall to Melanie's spotless room before she could change her mind.

After careful thought, she decided not to ask Amber to join the committee—at least not yet. Like Richard, she was more interested in having fun than getting anything done. And Tara wanted the committee to move fast.

Within twenty minutes, Tara had called up four people she believed would be good workers and still keep their mouths shut. Her committee had to be small, she figured, to keep Miss Dalton's fate a secret as long as necessary. All four agreed to help.

The Save Miss Dalton Committee's first meeting was planned for the next afternoon at Tara's house. At four-thirty on Friday, Tara and the S.M.D.C. gathered in her family room. After the air popper spewed out two tubfuls of popcorn, Tara passed around bowls and glasses of canned fruit punch.

"This meeting is now in order." She glanced at the clock. "My folks get home from work in half an hour, and you guys have to be gone by then. So listen up."

When she finally had Oliver's and Peter's attention, she asked, "First, do you guys understand why you're sworn to secrecy?"

Vicki looked at Tara, at the nodding boys, and back to Tara again. "I don't," she whispered, shaking her head.

Tara was glad Vicki had come. She didn't say much, but she'd be a hard worker. Evidently she didn't hold a grudge. "We have to keep our activities quiet for two reasons. First, the news isn't official yet. Miss Dalton doesn't even know about it. We don't want her to accidentally hear about losing her job. Second, a surprise attack on the enemy is always best."

Karin munched her popcorn one kernel at a time. "When *do* we go public?"

"Within a week." Tara glanced over her shoulder, but Rhett had gone outside with his Yo-Yo. "I sent a letter about Miss Dalton to the editor of the *Chronicle*. I'm hoping it will be printed next week."

"So we'll be ready with our plan of action the day it appears in the paper?" Karin asked.

Tara nodded, glad she'd asked Karin to join them. So far she'd been surprisingly nice. Tara still suspected

Karin didn't like her very much, but they did have one thing in common. They both wanted Miss Dalton to keep her job.

Oliver scratched his stomach. "What *is* our strategy, exactly?"

Tara glanced at her list. "First of all, each one of us will write up a petition at home. As soon as my letter is printed, we'll go door-to-door collecting signatures."

Peter crunched his ice cubes. "What if they don't print your letter?"

"I thought of that." Tara handed out paper and pencils. "Even if the letter isn't published, we'll go into action next Friday, one week from today."

Karen leaned over the map Tara opened. "What's this for?"

"To assign sections of town for when we begin collecting signatures. We don't want to cover the same blocks. It's a small town—we should be able to hit most of it." She'd already divided the town into five areas.

"Then what?" Oliver asked, peering at the map. He stabbed his pencil through a street name. "That's where I live."

"After our petitions are filled, Amber will give them to her dad." She lowered her voice. "But, remember, mum's the word. If Amber's dad heard how we found out about Miss Dalton losing her job, he'd kill her."

"No!" Oliver clasped his hand over his heart. "Then I'd have to take over for her in the play!" He jumped on top of the coffee table and did six quick tap dance steps.

"Knock it off, Oliver." Tara held up the map. "See where I've written your names? That's your section to cover. Maybe you should write down the boundary lines of your area." She glanced at the clock. 5:10. "And hurry up. My parents will be home in five minutes." Tara didn't feel ready yet to explain to her mom what the committee was planning.

While the committee members took notes, Tara dumped the dirty glasses into the popcorn bowl. She ran upstairs and loaded the dishwasher. Since she and Melanie did the supper dishes, her mom would never know anyone else had been there.

When her mom and dad pulled into the driveway ten minutes later, the S.M.D.C. members were gone, the popcorn hulls picked up, and Tara was in her room. She thought the first committee meeting had gone well. Everyone seemed willing to work hard, but time was awfully short. If only they could do enough!

On Monday morning Tara's mind was filled with the S.M.D.C. plans. It was hard being around Amber, but she knew she couldn't tell her best friend yet. Amber couldn't always keep a secret, and Tara didn't dare take a chance.

Amber didn't seem to notice her silence. She hopped up and down the sidewalk after lunch, practicing her routine. "I brought my tap shoes to school," she said, holding up a drawstring bag. "Miss Dalton wants me to rehearse the intermission this afternoon."

Nodding absent-mindedly, Tara followed Amber into class. Karin and two boys were setting up the wagon they'd finished painting. The janitor rolled an ancient piano into the room, waved, and left again. Pushing a cart on wheels, Oliver brought in seven foil-covered rocks, placing them in the middle of the "river."

Tara clasped her hands together. Things were really shaping up! This was, without a doubt, going to be the best Sixth Grade Drama Night ever.

Glancing at Miss Dalton, Tara just hoped it wouldn't be the *last* Sixth Grade Drama Night.

Suddenly a thundering "dum-dum-de-dum, DUM, DUM" echoed from the piano. Miss Dalton, grinning, motioned for everyone to sit down.

"For your entertainment pleasure, Miss Amber Mc-Cubbin will perform for you her own rendition of 'Way Down upon the Suwannee River.'" Miss Dalton swung her arm out to the right. "Take it away, Amber!"

After a snappy introduction, Amber burst out from

behind the piano. Although still in blue jeans and T-shirt, her tap shoes click-clicked like castanets across the wooden floor. Miss Dalton kept up a steady beat on the piano.

Arms swinging as she danced, Amber belted out her song. "Way down upon the Suwan*nee* Ri*ver*! Far, far away. That's where my heart is yearn*ing* ev*er*! That's where the old folks stay."

Tara sat forward. Amber'd been practicing, all right. She was really good! Tara hated to admit it, but Amber might add some pizazz to the show after all.

After a short piano interlude, Amber launched into the second verse. By the time she hit, "All the world is sad and weary, everywhere I roam. Oh, brother, how my heart *grows* wea*ry*," she had *tap-tap-tapped* to the front of the room. Abruptly, she stopped in midsentence.

"Oh, ugh!" She crouched down and the music stopped.

Miss Dalton stood and leaned over the top of the piano. "What's the matter?"

"Gum! Somebody left gum on the floor and it's all over my tap shoes! All right, who did this?" Amber swung to face Richard.

"Don't look at me." Richard held up both hands. "I don't throw gum on the floor. I stick it under my desk."

Amber glared at him, then pulled at the gluey gum. "How will I ever get this crud off?" she wailed. Long gooey strings looped from her fingers to her toes.

"Let me try." At her desk Miss Dalton pulled a small bottle of nail polish remover from the top drawer. "Best thing I've ever found for removing gum."

In less than a minute she cleaned the gum from Amber's shoes. "P-U!" Richard pinched his nostrils. The air reeked of nail polish remover.

"I'm sure you'll all now agree that Amber's dance idea was a good one," Miss Dalton said as she stood up. "Now, let's go on to the rehearsal."

Amber thudded in her stocking feet back to her desk, bowing and curtsying as she went. Sherman and Karin stood talking near the wagon. Tara watched them try different arrangements of the cardboard horse in front of the wagon. The cotton for Scene One lay in a heap on the floor.

Tara knew exactly how the wagon should be arranged to give the audience the best view of the hiding slaves. "Here, turn the horse like this so Jeremy can hide behind it while he wiggles the wagon. Then, with the wagon at an angle, the slaves can be seen better." She piled the cotton stuffing in the wagon. "Like this."

"Thanks." Nodding, Sherman called out, "Places, everybody!"

Tara collapsed Indian-style in front of Sherman's chair, waiting anxiously for the action to start. In today's rehearsal Jeremy would shake the wagon a little, to imitate a horse trotting as the fugitive slaves escaped through the woods. When the slave catchers jumped out, Tara was sure Peter would do a terrific job as John Fairfield, but she never knew what Richard would pull.

"Action!"

Hiding behind the horse, Jeremy leaned on the pole attached to the wagon, rocking it back and forth. Peter flapped imaginary reins while the slaves bobbed up and down under the stuffing.

Richard's face poked out through the cotton. " 'Iz this a dream? I canna believe I runned away.' "

Beverly clutched the doll. " 'Ef we stay, dey kill us sooner or later,' " she predicted darkly. " 'I tarred of bakin' de bread and dey only gib us de cruss.' "

" 'Ah knows it. Jess the same,' " Richard said, " 'I allus been trusted. But now I is a runaway!' " With that, he beat his chest in agony, falling over on his back in the pile of stuffing. "Yee-oww!" Cotton flying, Richard scrambled to a sitting position again.

"Cut. Cut." Sherman stood tiredly. "What's wrong now?"

"Something stuck me, that's what!" Richard dug in the fluffy mounds of couch stuffing.

Beverly leaned over. After digging carefully through

the "cotton," she held up three long straight pins. "This is what got you. They were left in the cushions somehow."

"Not by accident, I'll bet." Richard pointed at Amber. "What a crummy thing to do! Just for a little gum on your dumb shoes."

"I didn't put those pins there!" Amber turned to Miss Dalton. "Honest, I didn't. I wasn't even up there."

Miss Dalton took the pins. "I'm sure there's a logical explanation for their being here. Before we continue, let's check through the rest of the stuffing."

Tara sighed and joined the group at the wagon. Just when the rehearsal was going well, another interruption. "Talk about trying to find a needle in a haystack," she muttered. She didn't think it was any easier in a pile of cotton.

Only two more pins were finally found, but searching used up the rest of the rehearsal time. Tara secretly watched the other kids while sorting through her pile of stuffing. Was somebody out to get Richard? First his script turned up missing, then he fell on the slick wet floor, and now the pins.

But why?

When the rest of the week's rehearsals went smoothly, Tara finally decided she'd been imagining things. On Friday, however, all thoughts of the play were pushed from her mind when her letter to the editor was printed in the *Chronicle*.

Miss Dalton walked into class that morning, carrying a copy of the newspaper. Statuelike, she waited until the whispering stopped. "I'm afraid I have some sad news." She paused and ran her long fingers through her curls. "Yesterday after school, I was informed that I would not be returning to Winchester Heights next year to teach."

Tara held her breath. The room buzzed with questions, but her eyes never left Miss Dalton's face.

"Of course, I was shocked and upset. Then, this morning at breakfast, I happened across a letter to the editor, asking the school board to reverse their decision." She walked down the aisle to lay the paper on Tara's desk. Smiling, she squeezed Tara's hand. "I will always be grateful for your support—all of you—at this time."

Tara stared down at the newspaper. It was folded open to the editorial page. Her eyes locked on the words, "Tara Brown, Chairperson of the Save Miss Dalton Committee."

When she glanced up, Miss Dalton was already pulling on rubber gloves to mix plaster of paris for the first science class. She winked at the class. "I *am* teaching today, however. Let's get started."

On her way to reading class, Tara cornered Karin. "Spread the word to the other S.M.D.C. members. Today after school, we take our petitions door to door."

"We're ready," Karin said. "I'll tell the others right after I feed the mice."

"Good."

On the way to Miss Button's room, Tara glanced at the newspaper still clutched in her hand. If Miss Dalton was grateful for their support already, just wait till she saw what else they had in store for the school board.

9

Surprise Ending

After Tara had covered four square blocks that afternoon, she'd collected twenty-two signatures on her petition. Each time she rang a doorbell, her plea for Miss Dalton's job grew more intense.

At five o'clock she turned toward home for supper, eager to tell her parents about the letter to the editor. She tried several times. However, during the salad her mom talked constantly about the new mirrors she was installing at her fitness club. Tara started to mention her letter after that, but her dad ranted all during the baked fish about the new higher quotas set by his sales manager.

Finally, during dessert, Tara cleared her throat. "Um, did anybody see today's paper?"

Her mom raised one eyebrow. "What?" she asked

vaguely. "Did you say something?" She sounded distracted and a little irritated.

Tara felt her face grow warm. She was almost sorry she'd said anything. "Oh, it was nothing," she muttered.

"Did you see Tara's great letter to the editor?" Melanie asked brightly. "Everybody was talking about it at school today."

"Yes, we read it at noon," Mr. Brown said. "Quite interesting."

Tara smiled at her dad and scooped up a bite of strawberry yogurt whip.

However, her mother frowned. "I don't understand why you'd want to get involved. It's really none of your business. You'll only get known as a troublemaker." She pointed her spoon at Tara. "Even if you don't care about your own reputation, you might think about us. How do you suppose this makes us look?"

Tara mushed up the rest of her yogurt and slumped in her chair. She should have known what her mother would think. As if Tara'd never spoken, her mom went on to discuss new colored lights that supposedly made the patrons feel cooler as they exercised.

"Excuse me," Tara said.

When nobody answered, she left the table. Upstairs on her bed, she reread the published letter, then her petition. She wished her parents thought this was important, but she suspected that that would never happen. How Tara *looked* was always more important to her mom than what she *did*. At least Melanie understood—that was something.

Five minutes later a soft knock sounded on Tara's door. "Who is it?"

"Just me." Melanie opened the door barely wide enough to slide through, then closed it softly. "Um, don't pay any attention to what Mom said. She doesn't know what a great teacher Miss Dalton is."

Tara shrugged. "It doesn't matter." Surprised, Tara realized it was true. Even if her mom disagreed with the S.M.D.C.'s activities, it was something she had to do. She held out her petition for Melanie to read. "I got twenty-two signatures this afternoon."

Melanie scanned the petition, then sat cross-legged on the bed beside Tara. "I know it doesn't help much, but I admire your guts. I could never have done this at your age."

The hard knot in Tara's stomach started to melt. "Thanks," Melanie."

After her sister left, Tara picked up the framed picture of Amber and her that sat on her desk. After removing their grinning faces, she replaced the photo with her published letter. Framed on her desk, the letter would be a constant reminder. She nodded with determination.

Even if her parents ignored her efforts, she would do all she could to keep Miss Dalton from leaving their school.

By Wednesday the members of the S.M.D.C. had covered the entire town. Tara presented Amber with the five signed petitions. "Deliver these to your dad tonight," she said.

"What are these?" Amber asked, thumbing through the sheets of paper.

"Petitions demanding that the school board give Miss Dalton her job back."

Amber shook her head slowly. "Aren't you getting carried away with this?"

"I don't believe you!" Tara jabbed at the petitions. "All these people here—more than two hundred names —agree with me."

"Look, my dad's just a member of the school board. Even if he agreed with you, he couldn't do anything. He's not that powerful." She tried to hand the petitions back.

Tara put her hands behind her back. "Come on. I'm not asking you to do anything but deliver them. *We* did all the work."

"Okay, but you're wasting your time." Amber stuck them in her locker. "I'll lug them home tonight."

But the next morning when Tara asked her what her dad had said about the petitions, Amber avoided her eyes. "I forgot to take them home. I'll remember tonight."

Tara fumed. On Friday morning she asked Amber the same question. "Will your dad call a special school board meeting since he's seen the petitions?"

"Um, well," Amber mumbled, digging to the back of her locker, "I didn't give the petitions to him yet."

"You said you took them home last night!"

"I did. I did." She slammed her locker shut. "But my folks had company last night and I went to bed before everyone left."

"You could have left the papers on his desk where he'd find them." Tara glared at her friend, hands on hips. "Are you *ever* going to give him those petitions?"

"All right, all right!" Amber lowered her voice as kids pointed at them and stared. "Don't have a heart attack. What's the big deal anyway? I'll give him the petitions this weekend."

"We don't have forever," Tara said, falling into step beside Amber on the way to music class.

"Why can't you give the petitions to him yourself?" Amber stared straight ahead. "I don't want to get caught in the middle of this stink."

"You're a real hero, Amber," Tara said sarcastically.

"I never said I *wanted* to be a hero." She stopped outside the music door. "I'll give Dad the petitions, but leave me out of your plans after this, okay? You take things too seriously. At our age, we're supposed to have fun."

Tara shook her head. Amber was the most fun kid in the class, but sometimes she seemed kind of hollow, like she didn't have any insides.

That afternoon during rehearsal, Tara's heart hammered as Elijah fought desperately with the slave catchers, trying to get his wife and children safely away. When Richard decided to be serious, he was a terrific actor. Tara decided Miss Dalton knew what she was doing after all when she chose him for the part.

Miss Dalton stopped by her desk, Lizzie's skirt in her hand. "The play is coming along well, don't you think?" she asked. "You should be proud. It's one of the best Drama Nights a sixth grade's ever produced."

As Miss Dalton moved down the aisle, Karin came from behind Tara and whispered. "Hey, you know something? We should get Miss Dalton some flowers."

"What for?"

"At real plays, somebody always gets a bouquet of roses after the final curtain."

"I think it's usually the star of the show who gets the flowers."

"Couldn't we get roses for Miss Dalton instead?"

Tara nodded slowly. "That *would* show our parents how much we like her. They'll know by then that Miss Dalton's losing her job."

"At least two members of the school board will be in the audience too," Karin added. "Amber's dad and

Peter's aunt are members. They'll probably both come
to the play."

When Karin left, Tara propped her chin on her fist.
She hadn't thought about any school board members
watching her play. Maybe she could take advantage of
that somehow. What if she made a short speech about
Miss Dalton's job when she gave her the bouquet?

Tara watched Miss Dalton at the back of the room.
She was everywhere: helping make reins for John Fairfield one minute, experimenting with make-up on Vicki
the next, then trying to fix Beverly's hair so it would fit
under a wig. She was always busy, yet never seemed
rushed, always having time if you needed help.

Tara made up her mind. She *would* do it!

At the end of the play, she'd ask Jake to play a drum
roll for her. Then she'd appear with the roses. Before
presenting them to Miss Dalton, she'd give a real tear-
jerker of a speech.

That night at home the speech was surprisingly easy
to write. Tara simply listed the reasons she felt Miss Dalton should keep her job. Finished at last, she bounded
downstairs to the family room.

In one corner, Rhett stood on a chair, trying to Walk
the Dog with his Yo-Yo. The dog wanted to jump more
than walk, but he was getting better. Her dad sat hunched

over his desk in the corner, while her mom practiced a new dance exercise routine to teach her club members.

"Want to hear my speech?" Tara called over the pulsating music.

"What?" her mom asked. "One, two, three, *kick*. One, two, three, *kick*."

Tara jumped out of range of her flying feet. "I said, DO YOU WANT TO HEAR MY SPEECH?"

"Step-together, step-together, hop, hop, hop." The pink leotard and tights flashed by.

Sighing, Tara turned to her dad, but didn't bother trying to get his attention. His hands were pressed over his ears as he studied the sheets of numbers spread out across his desk. Giving up, she plodded back up the stairs.

Passing Melanie's bedroom door, she decided to give her sister a try. That afternoon, when she'd told Melanie about the speech, her sister thought it was a good idea. Melanie opened on the third knock. "*What?*"

"You wouldn't want to hear the speech I'm giving at the end of Drama Night, would you?"

"Sure." She waved a hand through the air. "Can you do it while I paint my fingernails?"

"Okay. Here goes." Tara cleared her throat and rattled her papers. " 'Ladies and Gentlemen, thank you for your generous applause. The sixth grade class would now like to thank Miss Dalton, who made this production possible.' "

Melanie nodded and shook the bottle of polish. "Sounds okay so far."

" 'However, this may be the last Sixth Grade Drama Night to echo through the halls of Winchester Heights Elementary. As you may know, Miss Dalton's job has been cremated.' "

"Cremated?" Melanie dabbed at her thumbnail. "Do you mean terminated?"

"No. Cremated sounded more dramatic." When Melanie snickered, Tara hesitated, then scribbled in the word "terminated." Continuing with her speech, she listed things Miss Dalton had done, such as organizing the Bike-a-thon for cerebral palsy and heading the school ecology project the previous fall to clean up the town's only park.

" 'And in conclusion, Miss Dalton has been an inspiration to each student she's taught. She's a shining example to follow, a beacon of light in the darkness—' "

Melanie snorted. "Isn't that a little corny?"

"Well, maybe, but I want everyone—especially those board members—to be bawling by the time I finish. I want them to *beg* Miss Dalton to stay."

"But that line about the beacon of light is funny! People don't say things like that anymore. You'll have them rolling in the aisles instead of crying." Melanie blew on her wet nails. "I'd tone down that part at the end."

"You really think so?" At Melanie's nod, Tara slashed big X's through the last two lines.

Back in her room, Tara practiced again, trying to memorize her speech. She doubted she could flip speech cards and hold roses at the same time.

Studying herself in the mirror, Tara was horrified to discover that she licked her lips almost every other word. By the time she'd practiced her entire speech, she reminded herself of a hungry snake.

Striking a more casual pose, she leaned to the left with her hip jutted out. "That's no good," she mumbled. However, when she stood up straight to speak, she looked like a mannequin. Giving up, she collapsed backward on the bed.

"I need help," Tara muttered. Giving the speech wouldn't be so hard, she tried to convince herself. She just needed some pointers.

The next day, at the public library, Tara headed straight for Miss Henderson, the librarian.

"Yes, can I help you?" Miss Henderson pulled a sharpened pencil from behind her ear. The pencil had pink elephants all over it.

"I hope so." Tara glanced over her shoulder and whispered. "I have to give a speech, but I'm nervous. Just a little."

"I . . . see." Miss Henderson tapped her pencil eraser against her two tiny front teeth. "I think I know just the book. It's in the adult section—do you mind?"

"No, that's okay." Tara followed the librarian to the far corner of shelves.

Miss Henderson ran a long fingernail down the book spines, pulled out a book, and handed it to Tara. A man on the cover smiled at her from below the title: *Art Linkletter, Public Speaking for Private People.* Tara flipped it open and skimmed down the table of contents. Chapter Seven, "Making Friends With Your Audience," caught her eye.

"I'll take it. Thanks, Miss Henderson."

Tara checked out the book, then hurried home. Up in her room, she scanned the speech book. In "Making Friends With Your Audience," Tara found what she was looking for. She read slowly, trying to absorb the advice.

" 'An important element in speaking is your gestures,' " Mr. Linkletter said. " 'The basic rule to remember is this: the bigger your audience, the broader your gestures.' "

Tara leaned back on her elbows. "*That's* my problem," she said. Using no gestures at all had given her that dead look.

She read on about different gestures to use during speeches. She could point a finger at the audience, point a finger at herself, open her arms wide to stress a major point, or pound one fist against the palm of her other hand.

With these things in mind, Tara practiced her speech in front of the mirror again, her notes propped up on her dresser. Whenever possible, she included hand and arm movements.

"The sixth grade class would now like to thank Miss Dalton, who made this production possible." Tara flung her left arm toward an invisible Miss Dalton.

"However, this may be the *last* production to grace the halls of Winchester Heighs Elementary," she exclaimed, throwing both arms wide this time.

Her voice rose as she listed the reasons why Miss Dalton was the best teacher she'd ever had. When she proclaimed that "Miss Dalton has been an inspiration to each student she's taught," Tara clasped her hands together over her heart and stared heavenward.

At the end of the speech, Tara reread the part Melanie had laughed at, then snapped her fingers. There was nothing wrong with those lines—they just needed the right gestures.

Tara cleared her throat, then raised her left arm high in the air. She pointed her finger and stared at the ceiling. Her voice rose dramatically: "Miss Dalton is a shining example to follow . . . a beacon of light . . . in the darkness."

Her voice echoed in the silent room. It was perfect,

Tara decided as she dropped her Statue of Liberty pose. In fact, she'd almost brought tears to her *own* eyes.

She grinned at herself in the mirror. After this inspired speech, the school board would simply have to reverse its decision.

❧ 10 ❧

Sabotage

B ut I told you we'd use make-up for the play!" Tara
shouted at Beverly Monday morning. "You look—
You look—" Words failed her.

"You look orange," Amber finished flatly.

"What happened to your face?" Tara demanded.
"You can't get up on stage looking like that!"

"Nothing happened to my face," Beverly snapped.
"Mom wouldn't let me use her sun lamp after all, so I
used some Super-Tan yesterday. You know—the lotion
that makes you tan without the sun."

Tara sighed. "Your head looks like a pumpkin. Can't
you get rid of that orange color?" She peered closely.
"Can you scrub it off?"

"No, I can't!" Beverly punched Tara's shoulder. "It's

your fault anyway. My natural tan was already dark enough to play Lizzie."

The buzzer rang before Tara could answer. Beverly tossed her yellow hair back from her orange face, then flounced into the school building.

Amber shrugged. "No sweat. The play's not till Friday night. That gives her five days for it to wear off."

"I know." Tara stubbed her toe on the cement step. "I'm sick of Beverly, that's all. She never listens to anybody."

That afternoon, Miss Dalton sat on top of the piano and kicked her shoes off. "Drama Night's coming right up, gang. The play's progressing nicely, but we'll have to hit it hard this week in order to do a super job on Friday."

As if on cue, Sherman walked to the front of the room. "Let's start with the first scene then, and go straight through." He pointed at Amber. "Including the intermission."

Richard, Beverly, Vicki, Peter, and the two slave catchers hurried to the front of the room and took their places. Jeremy hid behind the cardboard horse.

"Action!" Sherman called out.

As Jeremy rocked the wagon and Peter flapped the reins, Beverly and Richard went through their lines. Tara jumped to her feet. "Wait, you guys!"

Sherman turned slowly. "What now?"

"It's time to try it without the scripts. They need to practice without the lines in their hands." Tara caught Beverly's scowl. "They've had plenty of time to learn their lines," she added.

"*I* know my lines," Beverly interrupted. "I like to carry my script, just in case."

Tara gritted her teeth. "I'll prompt you if you forget anything."

"Sherman?" Miss Dalton hopped down from the piano. "I do think Tara's right. It would be a good idea to practice without the scripts from now on. I should have mentioned it myself."

"Sure, Miss Dalton." Sherman collected the scripts and tossed them on the floor. "Anything else, Tara?" he asked. When she shook her head, he called out again, "Action!"

Through the first scene, Tara skimmed the lines of her new script copy. However, she only had to prompt Richard once, and Oliver twice. They knew their lines better than she'd even hoped. Amber's tap dance went off without a hitch, launching them into the second scene. Tara flipped page after page, following the actors' lines.

" 'The boats has stopped runnin'!' " Lizzie cried at the bank of the frozen river.

In last week's rehearsals, Beverly had practiced jumping from one foil-covered rock to another. But this time, under her long skirt, she wore the hoops Amber had made. The doll clutched under her arm, Beverly swayed as she started across.

However, with hoops on, Beverly kept missing the rocks. With each leap, the hoops swung up high in front of her, hiding the "river" from view. She had to guess where the rocks were, and usually she guessed wrong.

When Tara stood to protest, she caught Amber's grin across the room. Tara shut her mouth, then grinned back. It *was* funny, watching Beverly's orange face bobbing along above those ridiculous hoops.

However, by the time they'd started the scene over six times so Beverly could get across in her hoops, it wasn't funny anymore. With her best effort, she only crossed four of the seven ice floes before falling off.

Tara tapped Sherman on the back. "Those hoops aren't going to work. She can't see where she's going. I knew it was a dumb idea."

Sherman watched Beverly fall once again into the raging blue construction paper. "Give her one more chance."

Tara tapped her foot impatiently. "Come on, come *on*," she muttered.

Beverly backed up to the shore for one more try. She studied the rocks, lifted her hoops, then dashed across the ice, the baby dangling from one hand. One rock, two, then three. On the third rock, she swayed and flapped her arms, but regained her footing.

With a leap, she reached the fourth, fifth, and sixth rocks. Smirking, she hopped to the seventh and final ice floe. When her feet hit the foil, the ice floe tilted, dumping Beverly into the river.

"Ouww!" she yelled, landing on her back. Her hoops stood up vertically as she lay on the floor. *"Who moved that rock?"*

While Richard hauled Beverly to her feet, Tara hurried to check out the seventh rock. It looked all right to her, no more wobbly than ever. For a minute, she'd been afraid someone had played another prank. She sighed with relief. The play didn't need any more jinxes.

"Oh, no! I bent the hula hoop!" When Beverly stood, her skirt poked out at any odd angle. "Can you fix it like it was, Amber?"

Amber tied her tap shoes. "Probably, so don't flip your switch. Come on. I'll work on it in the restroom."

Oh well, Tara thought, they'd almost made it straight through the play. Of course, more drama was yet to come . . . Tara's mind wandered as she tried to imagine the audience's reaction when she appeared on stage after the play and sprung her surprise speech.

So far, she'd told no one but Melanie about it, not

even the committee. Jake only knew he was to play a drum roll at the end of the play before Tara presented the flowers.

Ten minutes later, a movement at the door caught Tara's eye. Beverly waltzed in, but Amber hung back and jerked her head sharply. "Come here," she whispered.

Just then, the final bell rang. Students stampeded for the door.

Amber pushed through the crowd and grabbed Tara's arm. "Come on." She steered her out the door and down the hall, melting into the crowd. At the restroom door she pulled Tara inside. Amber washed her hands and fixed her hair for five minutes until the room emptied.

"What are you being so mysterious about?" Tara demanded.

"I think you were right about someone sabotaging your play."

"What do you mean?"

"Remember how you thought somebody took Richard's script? And then dribbled water on the floor so he'd fall? And put pins in the couch stuffing?" Amber perched on the edge of the sink.

"I'm not so sure anymore." Tara leaned against the wall, sliding down till she rested on the floor.

"Well, you might have been right after all. While I was fixing Beverly's hoops, she accidentally let something slip. I think I know who your jinx is."

"It's Beverly? That twit. Somehow it doesn't surprise me."

"No, it's not Beverly, but she *was* mad because you didn't like her orange face. Anyway, she said she wasn't the only one bugged at you."

Tara rubbed her forehead as a tight knot formed in her stomach. "Who else is mad?"

"Sherman." Amber hopped down from the sink and sat beside Tara. "Beverly said he's mad because you try to direct the play."

"I do not!" Tara bristled. "I just help. I *am* the assistant."

"I know. I'm just telling you what Sherman told Beverly."

Just then a tiny girl came in and peeked in both sinks. "Did you see my spelling paper?" Her voice was as small as she was. "I got a sticker on it."

Tara smiled at her, but wished she'd leave. "No, we didn't see it."

After the little girl hunted through the garbage can, she gave up and left. As the door clicked shut, Tara demanded, "What else did Sherman say?"

"That his play was better, no matter what you said

was wrong with it. And that he didn't care if your play bombed or not." Amber shined her tap shoes with a paper towel. "*He* went along with Beverly wearing a hoop skirt, and you know what a pain that's been."

"True." Tara tried to imagine quiet Sherman Tool wrecking her play, but she couldn't. "Sherman's been nice to me. It doesn't sound like something he'd do. In fact, it sounds a lot more like Beverly to me."

"There's one way we could find out."

"How?"

"By searching Sherman's desk. If we find Richard's missing script there, we'll know it's Sherman who's been messing things up. He could have fixed it so the rock would tilt this afternoon too."

"We'd get caught if we tried to search his desk," Tara said, shaking her head. "Anyway, I don't believe anything Beverly says."

"Couldn't hurt to check." Amber stood and pulled Tara to her feet. "Come on. The room should be empty by now. You stand guard in the hall, and I'll search his desk."

The hallway was deserted. Amber removed her tap shoes and they tiptoed back to their room. The lights were already off, and the door was shut.

Amber turned the knob and the door swung open. "You wait here. Call if you see someone."

Tara leaned against the door frame, trying to look casual. Except for a teacher's aide who went by with a stack of worksheets, no one passed. Tara could hear Amber inside, rustling papers as she searched Sherman's desk.

Suddenly Tara stiffened. The principal was heading down the hall toward her. She had to warn Amber.

"Uh, HI, MR. WINSOR!" she yelled, stepping away from the door.

"Hello, Tara. Shouldn't you be out of the building?" His voice was frosty.

"I was just leaving! Amber forgot her tap shoes! She wants to practice her routine at home tonight!"

Mr. Winsor raised one pointy eyebrow. "You don't have to shout."

Tara smiled sickly, praying Amber had picked up her message. In ten seconds, Amber trotted out, swinging her tap shoes and humming. "Oh, hi, Mr. Winsor," she said, wide-eyed with surprise. "I was just getting my tap shoes."

"So I heard." He pivoted like a soldier, then started down the hall. "Run along home now, girls."

Tara swallowed her giggles until they reached their lockers, then bent double laughing. "I thought I was going to die when I saw him coming."

"Shh! Let's get out of here." Amber grabbed her

jacket and books, then followed Tara outside. Slipping around the corner of the building, Amber reached under her sweater and pulled out some papers.

When Tara saw the printed sheets, she knew. "Richard's old script?"

"Yup. It was buried at the bottom of Sherman's desk."

"I guess you were right." Tara shook her head. "Do you believe he caused all those other problems too?"

"I don't think that's important right now." Amber turned and faced Tara. "You should be worrying about what he may pull Friday night during the real performance."

Tara's hands grew clammy. "You don't really think he'd—"

"I don't know. It depends on how mad he is. But you'd better keep your eyes open." She studied the bottoms of her tap shoes. "I will too. I bet that turkey dropped the gum that got on my shoes last week. If he tries that again, I'm going to tap dance right across his face."

Tara nodded, barely hearing. She couldn't believe it! Sherman didn't act like the traitor type. Her stomach knotted painfully. What if he was saving his worst tricks for the real performance? It gave her a whole new set of problems to worry about. Her dream of producing a perfect play seemed more and more impossible.

However, Friday night arrived with no more rehearsal accidents. Tara tried to watch Sherman without being obvious, and was careful to offer no more suggestions when he was directing.

She split her time that week between worrying about Sherman and worrying about her speech. Each night Tara practiced her speech in front of her mirror. She memorized the words; by Friday the pointing and arm throwing felt more natural. During the play Friday night, she stood backstage, mumbling the words to herself over and over.

The first scene was applauded enthusiastically, even though Oliver had knocked over one of the trees while hiding behind it. Fifteen minutes later, Amber's tap dance to "Suwannee River" was received with whistles and cheers. At the end, flushed with excitement, Amber joined Tara backstage. "How's it going?" she whispered.

"Really good." Tara peered through the curtains.

So far, no one had forgotten his lines or missed a cue. But, while Tara watched, Beverly slipped off two ice floes as she swayed across the dangerous river. Tara held her breath until Beverly actually made it to the far river bank. At least she hadn't actually fallen down. That was something to be thankful for, Tara admitted as she dropped the curtain back into place.

"Where are Miss Dalton's roses?" Amber whispered.

"Over in that corner," Tara said, pointing. "Only

they're not roses. They're carnations. The money I collected would only buy four roses, but I could get eight carnations for the same price."

As a hush fell over the audience, the girls turned toward the stage. A limping Lizzie, tears running down her face, collapsed on the river bank. Clutching the baby in her arms, Beverly rocked back and forth, moaning. " 'Oh, Elijah! Oh, Mandy! I fear you are daid.' " She broke down and sobbed.

Tara grinned. When Beverly put her mind to it, she could be pretty convincing.

Struggling to her feet, Lizzie wrapped the doll tighter in the blanket. Tara listened, spellbound, as she delivered her final lines. " 'But you an' me, li'l one, we are alive!' " Her face glowing, Lizzie stumbled stage left. " 'Dey cain't keep us down no mo'e. We are alive—and free!' "

There was total silence for several seconds, then the audience erupted into applause. Tara joined in. She couldn't believe what a touching performance Beverly had given.

"Hey, get the flowers!" Amber hissed, elbowing her in the ribs.

Tara gasped. She'd forgotten. The curtain was closing and she could already hear movement in the audience. She grabbed the flowers, calling, "Jake! Let's hear it!"

Running to the side of the stage, she waited until the audience noticed the drum roll and settled back into their seats. Then, her knees shaking, Tara walked out onto the stage.

"Ladies and gentlemen," she began, "thank you for your generous applause. The sixth grade class would now like to thank Miss Dalton, who made this production possible."

Cheers came from the cast as Miss Dalton climbed the steps to the stage. Smiling, she crossed to where Tara held out the carnations.

"Thank you. They're lovely." She faced the audience. "This has been a fun class to work with. I enjoy Drama Night as much as they do."

Before anyone could move, Tara stepped forward to the very edge of the stage, as close to the audience as possible. Their shuffling and squirming was drowned out by her pounding heart.

"We're glad you've enjoyed this evening," she began slowly. "However, this may be the last Sixth Grade Drama Night to ever echo through the halls of Winchester Heights Elementary." She flung her arms wide. "As you may know, Miss Dalton's job has been terminated."

Someone behind her gasped. Tara stiffened her wobbly knees, determined to finish. She spotted her parents halfway back and faltered as her mother shook her head disgustedly.

Ignoring her, Tara focused her eyes on the auditorium's far door and proclaimed, "Miss Dalton has been an inspiration to each student she's taught."

Point by point, her voice rose as she listed the reasons to keep Miss Dalton. She pointed her finger toward the ceiling and stared at the rafters. "We must not let teachers like Miss Dalton leave Winchester Heights. She is a shining example to follow." Her voice dropped almost to a whisper. "A beacon of light . . . in the darkness."

She dropped her arm; her head hung down.

The lights were dimmed in the total silence. Then one of the students behind Tara whistled. Clapping and feet stomping followed, low at first, then loud enough to shake the stage. One by one, the parents in the audience stood and joined the students.

Turning, Tara saw Miss Dalton walking slowly toward her. She put an arm around Tara and pulled her close. The carnations were crushed between them.

11

The S.M.D.C. Strikes Again

After the applause died down, Tara moved in a daze to find her parents. Strangers reached out as she came down the stage steps and said, "Great speech!" Others nodded or smiled as she worked her way through the milling people.

Halfway back she spotted Rhett swinging his Yo-Yo and waving from where he stood on a chair. "Hey, Tara! It was neat!"

"Thanks." She lifted him down to the floor.

Melanie grinned, her braces sparkling. "Way to go, Miss Playwright. I must admit it turned out terrific. I hope you told everyone I typed it."

Tara only half-listened to Melanie's words while she waited for her parents to finish talking to Peter's dad.

When they did finally turn toward her, neither one mentioned her speech.

"Ready to go?" her dad asked. "I'll go get the car. That was a nice play, honey," he added before darting through the crowd.

Tara's mother nodded absently. "Yes, very nice, dear," she said, not quite meeting Tara's eyes. "It's too bad Beverly fell off the ice floes, though." She smiled frostily over Tara's head, nodding at someone behind her.

Turning away, Tara felt the sting of tears behind her eyelids. Trust her mom to notice what went *wrong* with the play. She tried not to feel deflated. Even if her mom wasn't impressed, other people seemed to have liked the performance. Anyway, Tara figured, she was probably just mad about the speech. In her mom's eyes, it no doubt took some of the shine off the perfect impression she was supposed to create.

Melanie tapped her on the arm. "Say, what are you going to do to celebrate? After all, this *is* your first play. By the way, would you autograph my program?"

Tara appreciated Melanie's cheery words, but her attention was drawn to Amber and her parents who were coming toward her. Amber, still in her tights and sequined outfit, looked uncomfortable.

Amber's father walked up to Tara with a tight-lipped expression. "Good evening, Tara," he said formally. "That was quite a speech just now. The petitions were impressive also." He smiled thinly. "What form of protest can I look forward to next?"

Before Tara could answer, her mom broke in smoothly. "She just got carried away with that speech. Childish enthusiasm, you know. But I'm sure that will be all, won't it, Tara?"

"I don't know," Tara mumbled, staring at the floor.

She clenched her fists. Even if her mom and Mr. McCubbin hadn't liked the speech, Miss Dalton had. She'd thanked her over and over, saying she'd remember it always. Hoping for Amber's help, Tara glanced at her best friend, who merely shrugged and looked the other way. Tara sighed. She should have known Amber wouldn't get involved.

"These protests *do* look rather childish," Mr. McCubbin continued, peering down his nose at Tara. "You obviously don't understand budget cuts. Regardless of my feelings about Miss Dalton, there's nothing I can do to save her job."

Rhett yanked on his mother's sleeve. "Hey, where's the bathroom?"

"I'll go with you," Tara interrupted quickly, glad for an excuse to get away from Mr. McCubbin.

"I'll come too," Amber said.

They took Rhett to the boys' restroom, then waited in the corridor. "Sorry about my dad," Amber said. "He didn't seem that upset about your speech. But then

Vicki's mom told him maybe *you* should have a seat on the school board too."

"That's okay. I just hope the speech did some good."

At that moment, Tara heard Miss Dalton's low chuckle. Coming toward them, she carried her carnations and talked with a parent on each side of her. When she spotted Tara, she broke away from the parents.

"Congratulations, Tara! The play was a hit! I've heard so many lovely comments from parents and students both. This is the best turnout we've ever had, thanks to having extra seating in the auditorium." She handed Tara and Amber each a carnation. "And your tap dance was terrific, Amber! You never missed a step."

Remembering her mom's words, Tara sighed. "I just wish Beverly hadn't slipped off the rocks. I guess it really spoiled the scene."

"Good heavens, not at all," Miss Dalton said. "It was hardly noticeable. People were sitting on the edges of their seats, waiting to see if Lizzie was going to escape." She waved to more parents. "When she almost dropped the baby in the river, you could have heard a pin drop. Believe me, Tara, the audience loved it." She gently squeezed Tara's arm before moving on down the hallway.

Then Richard and Peter, still in costume, sauntered past on their way to the classroom. Watching them, Tara was suddenly sorry the play was over. The rehearsals *had* been fun, in spite of Richard's clowning and Beverly's temper tantrums. And Miss Dalton was positive tonight's performance had been a real success.

Smelling the delicate pink carnation, Tara compared her mom's and Miss Dalton's reactions to the play. They'd both seen the exact same performance. Her teacher was sure the audience had loved it, yet her mom only saw it as "less than perfect." Evidently Miss Dalton didn't think something had to be perfect in order to be good, and Tara had a lot of respect for her teacher's ideas.

Tara lifted her chin. It was time to stop worrying about always being the best; otherwise, straining to be perfect would ruin everything she enjoyed. She might as well face facts. Most likely, she'd never live up to her mom's expectations. Maybe it was time to stop trying so hard, and just do what she thought was most important.

She straightened her shoulders and grinned. "Perfect or not, here I come!"

"What?" Amber asked.

"Nothing." Tara grabbed Amber's arm. "Melanie said I should celebrate, so let's have a party! I bet Dad would let me invite some of the kids over for pizza. It won't take long to clean the auditorium. Mr. Winsor said I just have to make sure the programs and litter are picked up and thrown away."

Amber scuffed one tap shoe back and forth on the tile. "Oh, I don't know. Everybody's probably too tired for a party. I know I am," she said, staring at the floor.

"I'm not tired. I'm too wound up to sleep for hours and hours. I bet the others feel the same way." Tara ticked off names on her fingers. "Let's see, I could ask Karin and Vicki, and Peter and Oliver and Richard. With you and me, that makes—"

"I wouldn't do that." Amber sighed, then looked directly at Tara. "They can't come."

"How do you know?"

"Most of them are going to Beverly's for a cast party." She turned as Rhett came out of the restroom. "I'll come to your house though."

Holding Rhett's hand, Tara started down the hall-way. Her voice sounded flat. "Were you invited to Bev-erly's?"

"Yes, but probably just because I fixed those hoops for her." She shrugged and yawned. "Who wants to go to Beverly's house, anyway? I sure don't."

Tara knew Amber would normally have jumped at the chance to go. "Just because she didn't invite me, you don't need to miss her party."

At the door of the auditorium, Rhett broke loose and raced down the nearly empty aisle to where Amber's parents still stood with Tara's mom. Tara collapsed into a seat in the last row, with Amber beside her.

Tara folded her program neatly in half. "You know something? I don't really understand why Beverly doesn't like me. She was glad enough to get a leading part in *Smuggled to Safety.*"

And without me, Tara added silently, *there wouldn't have even been a play.* At least, not that one.

Amber rested her head on the back of the seat. "Beverly's used to getting her own way. You had the nerve to complain about her orange face and weird umbrella skirt."

"I was only trying to help. She should have listened to me about the make-up. And I warned her she'd trip in those hoops, which she did." She scrunched down in the padded seat. "I was *right* about doing it my way."

"Sure," Amber said, "but to Beverly, that just makes it worse."

Tara pulled herself to her feet. "I guess we're leaving now." Her mom was coming up the aisle, Melanie and Rhett beside her.

"I'll come home with you if you still want me to," Amber offered. "We could celebrate by ourselves. I'll make my sauerkraut pizza."

Tara shuddered and stuck out her tongue. "Yuck." Stretching, she faked a yawn. "Maybe another time. I guess I'm more tired than I thought."

Tara spent the weekend with her feelings riding a roller coaster. Sometimes she felt high, remembering the applause after the play and Miss Dalton's hug after her speech. Other times, she wanted to crawl under her bed and hide, thinking about Beverly's cast party.

By Monday morning, she'd hidden away her play program and was determined to concentrate on helping Miss Dalton. She pulled Karin aside as they went into the building. "Pass the word to the rest of the committee. There's a meeting today after school at my house."

That afternoon the five members gathered in Tara's kitchen. Tara'd bought a box of Oreos on the way home, which she set in the middle of the table beside a carton of milk.

"Okay, the S.M.D.C. meeting is now called to order. First, don't get cookie crumbs on the floor or I'll catch it later. Also, you only get one glass of milk each." She passed around the cups.

"What's the meeting for?" Peter asked, dipping a cookie into his milk.

"We need some new ideas for saving Miss Dalton's job. We've used the editorial, the petitions, and the speech after the play." Tara tapped her pencil on the table. "What haven't we tried yet?"

Oliver pulled his four Oreos apart and picked out the frosting. "How about making a commercial? You know, like those campaign commercials you see before elections?"

"Great idea!" Peter said.

"No way." Tara shook her head. "That would cost a ton of money, for one thing. Anyway, what do you know about making commercials?"

"What about making posters to put up around town?" Karin asked.

Tara nodded, writing *posters* on her note pad. "Good. What else?"

Vicki nibbled on a cookie, reminding Tara of Limburger, the mouse. "Um, well, we could do something just before the school board meeting next week."

Tara hesitated, remembering Mr. McCubbin's nasty remarks after the play. "What exactly did you have in mind?"

"I don't know," Vicki mumbled, shrinking back in her chair. "What about a parade, or, or . . . something?"

Tara glanced at the small group around the table. "Five people wouldn't make a very impressive parade. Plus, if it rained, the parade would have to be cancelled. I bet we'd even have to get a permit to march in the street."

Vicki slipped down further in her chair, brushing the crumbs from her lips. Rhett zoomed through, grabbed two cookies, hit Tara on the leg with his Yo-Yo, then zoomed out again.

"Any other ideas?" Tara asked. When no one spoke up, she said, "I guess making posters is the next step, then. If we all make two big posters to display around town, lots of people should see them, including the board members."

For five minutes they discussed where to put the posters. At ten past five, Tara grabbed the milk and put it in the refrigerator. "Sorry, but my mom gets home in ten minutes. You guys better go."

In two minutes she had the empty cookie container and paper cups in the wastebasket and the table wiped off. In three more minutes she had all four committee members out the door. Tara knew her mom's opinion of the S.M.D.C., and she didn't want to put her friends through a lecture.

"Keep thinking of more ideas!" she called after the committee before shutting the door.

Melanie emerged from the living room. "Get a lot done?"

"Not really." Tara read her short list. "Karin thought of making posters, and we're going to do that. The others came up with stuff that would never work, like having a parade or making a commercial." Tara started upstairs.

"A parade? What's wrong with a parade? You could get a lot of attention that way, I'd think."

"It wouldn't work." Tara sat on a step and picked at the shaggy carpet. "No one would notice such a small group. I doubt if we could march in the street without a permit either."

"Then couldn't you march on the sidewalk? You could carry big banners. People would notice you if someone played a drum or bugle." She stepped around Tara and started up the stairs. Pausing, she turned. "You know," Melanie said, "I think you're a good leader. You try hard and you're organized."

"Thanks," Tara said, turning around to smile at her older sister. "I do work hard—"

"But part of being a leader is listening to others," Melanie interrupted. "Other people have good ideas too." Melanie's smile softened her words before she disappeared down the hall.

Tara rested her chin in her hands, surprised at what Melanie had to say. Was her sister right? She hadn't really given Vicki's parade idea any serious thought. In her opinion, it wouldn't work, so she'd brushed it aside.

On the other hand, speaking her mind seemed to be causing her trouble lately. She'd been against Amber's tap dance for the intermission, yet it had been a real hit.

And there was Sherman. She'd only been trying to help him direct the play; he'd seen it as being bossy, though, and almost sabotaged the whole thing.

She'd even made Peter mad about the program. She'd thought her suggestions about the artwork would be helpful, but she must have sounded more critical than she'd meant to.

And, of course, there was always Beverly. However,

Tara decided, Beverly was just a grouch. Her orange face *had* looked weird, and the hoop skirt *had* made her fall off the rocks. Beverly didn't like anyone to tell her anything. In Beverly's case, Tara knew it wouldn't have mattered how nice she'd sounded.

But Melanie's words still made sense. Other people *did* have good ideas. Maybe she'd turned down Vicki's idea without enough reason.

Just then Tara heard the family car pull into the driveway. She scooted up the stairs and down the hall to her parents' bedroom. Sitting on the bed by the telephone, she flipped through the phone book and dialed.

The phone was picked up after the first ring. "Vicki? I've been thinking about your parade idea. On second thought, I think it could work." She bounced lightly on the bed, curling the cord around her finger. "What exactly did you have in mind?"

❧ 12 ❧

The Parade

Laughing kids gathered in the warm April evening, waving signs and banners. Weaving through the crowd on the sidewalk, Jake beat a loud tattoo on his snare drum.

Tara grabbed Richard's arm as he sauntered past. "Blow your trumpet. Loud," she added. "It's almost six-thirty and time to get the parade started."

After Richard blasted his horn twice in the still air, the parade members drifted into place. Tara balanced on Richard's trumpet case in front of the group.

"Line up, everybody!" she shouted. "The school board meeting starts in exactly thirty minutes! We must leave now to get to the school on time."

Vicki and Karin, carrying the SAVE MISS DALTON'S JOB! banner, snaked through the group to the front. Jake, with his snare drum, Richard, with his trumpet, and Beverly, with her saxophone, lined up directly behind the banner.

When Tara had asked at school for volunteers to march in the parade, eight other kids agreed to join them. They all carried signs taped to yardsticks. Peter's poster was a giant picture of Miss Dalton drawn by his dad. Under Miss Dalton's smiling face were the words "We Need Her!"

Tara, at the front of the parade, raised her baton high. When it came down, Jake struck up a stirring cadence. The sixth graders cheered, then started down the sidewalk. Oliver started to chant, *"Left, right, left, right,* I *left* my wife and *forty*-eight children, in a *starving* condition with*out* any gingerbread *left."*

"Cut! Cut!" Tara sliced her baton through the air. "You're supposed to be shouting *'Save Miss Dalton's Job!'* Now, let's hear it!"

They marched the eight blocks to the high school, taking small steps so people could read their signs. At first, few people were outside to notice them. But as they neared the town square where people shopped, they began to draw a crowd.

In her best drum majorette style, Tara pumped her baton up and down, shouting, *"Save Miss Dalton's Job!"* Some people stared at them and shook their heads, while others cheered as they passed. Tara tried to ignore the junior high kids who laughed at them, but it was hard when a spit wad landed on her arm.

As they neared the end of their march, Tara's stomach tightened into a knot. The school board meeting was open to the public, but she was still afraid Amber's dad would get their group kicked out.

At exactly eight minutes before seven, they arrived at the high school entrance. Chanting while they marched in place, they didn't have long to wait before the first board members arrived.

Miss Knickerbocker, chairman of the board, strode right through them, never blinking. Mr. Dorr followed close behind her, but turned and winked before going into the building. Tara felt a surge of hope—maybe they had a friend there. When Mrs. Bromley, Peter's aunt, arrived, she waved and mussed up Peter's hair as she walked by.

However, when Amber's dad arrived, the air took on a frosty chill. Heart hammering, Tara chanted as loudly as her hoarse voice would allow: *"Save Miss Dalton's Job! Save Miss Dalton's Job!"*

Mr. McCubbin stalked through the group as if they were invisible. His lips in a thin line, he swept into the building without a backward glance.

After he disappeared, Tara waved her baton.

"Enough! Stop!" The noise died down abruptly. "Remember, we have to be quiet inside. If we're noisy, they can throw us out. It would get a lot of publicity, but it wouldn't help Miss Dalton's chances any."

The instruments and baton were parked inside the front doors, but the banner and posters were carried down the hall. In Room 318 where the meeting was to be held, Tara forced her wobbling legs to march to the empty front row of chairs.

Teacher contracts was the last item on the printed agenda, but the parade members waited quietly. After an hour of discussing additional cross-walk signs, new basketball uniforms, and cost estimates of getting the school bus fixed, Miss Knickerbocker cleared her throat noisily.

"We'll now move on to the subject of teacher contract renewals."

Mr. McCubbin peered over his reading glasses at Tara's group in the front row, as if expecting an uproar. He looked disappointed when they didn't start to riot.

Miss Knickerbocker leaned forward toward the students. "Let us assure you of one thing. We do understand your feelings about Miss Dalton."

"However, there's nothing we can do about her job," Mr. McCubbin interrupted. "There's not enough money, and that's all there is to it. Last hired, first fired. Miss Dalton's been here less time than the other teachers."

Peter's aunt waved a pen in the air. "Actually, Mr. McCubbin, we haven't seriously considered any other alternatives."

Amber's dad reared back, rocking his chair on its back legs. "There *aren't* any alternatives, Mrs. Bromley. There won't be any money for her salary next year."

"Maybe." Peter's aunt scanned a paper in front of her. "But then, maybe we could cut somewhere else in our budget. I've thought of some possibilities. Until these children brought their feelings to our attention, I had not seriously considered any other choice."

"Have you thought of something?" Miss Knickerbocker asked.

"I may have. I'm not sure yet." Peter's aunt smiled at the sixth graders, one by one. "It needs more study."

Karin nudged Tara. "Maybe Miss Dalton won't get fired after all," she whispered.

Twisting in her chair, Tara glanced over her shoulder. Miss Dalton didn't seem to be anywhere in the room.

Mr. McCubbin's icy voice cut crisply through the room. "I sincerely doubt there is any real chance of keeping Miss Dalton in our school system." He scowled at Peter's aunt.

"However," Miss Knickerbocker cut in, "the board will discuss Mrs. Bromley's ideas further this week, then make its final decision public."

Tara let out the breath she'd been holding and slumped in her chair. She'd really hoped the board would decide something that night. Soon Miss Knickerbocker adjourned the meeting, and Tara's group filed out slowly. Karin's parents gave her and Vicki a ride home.

Letting herself in the kitchen door, Tara found her mom making a cup of hot tea. "Hi." She glanced in the living room. "Where is everybody?"

"Your dad's still at his business meeting. Melanie isn't home from the library yet." She stirred in her artificial sweetener. "How did the meeting go?"

"I don't really know. The school board is going to reconsider firing Miss Dalton. They'll announce their decision later this week."

"I doubt if they'll seriously consider what a bunch of sixth graders think." She rinsed her spoon. "I still don't think it was a good idea to get so involved. Melanie wouldn't have done this. Whatever prompted you to make a spectacle of yourself this way?"

Tired from the march and sick of being compared to Melanie, Tara snapped, "What I did was *important*. I really don't care if I looked like a spectacle or not."

"Well, you *should* care! You must think of your reputation!"

Tara backed up two steps and leaned heavily against the table. "My reputation?" she asked quietly. "Or yours?"

Her mom shook her head as she turned and left the room. "I just don't understand you."

Sighing, Tara had to agree. Her mom probably never *would* understand. But whether Miss Dalton got to keep her job or not, Tara wasn't sorry about what her committee had done.

She spoke to the empty room. "If I had to choose all over again, I'd still do the same thing."

Trying to squelch her letdown feeling, Tara trudged upstairs and took a steamy shower. Then, exhausted, she crawled into bed and fell deeply asleep.

For three days Tara and the S.M.D.C. pestered Amber to find out about the board's decision. Amber claimed she knew nothing about it, and wasn't going to ask. Tara gave up: how could Amber care so little? Especially with her dad on the school board.

On Friday morning when the final bell rang, Miss Dalton still hadn't appeared. Tara leaned across the aisle. "Karin, have you seen Miss Dalton this morning?"

Karin shook her head, but pointed to the teacher's desk. Miss Dalton's hand-knit sweater was draped over the back of her chair, as always.

Richard chomped on his gum, cracking and popping. "Maybe Miss Dalton's gone on strike," he said.

"Or maybe she's going to quit before they can fire her," Karin added.

"Morning, kids. Sorry I'm late."

Tara jumped as Miss Dalton pushed open the door and let it slam. Striding to the front of the room, she turned, a huge grin covering her face. "I have some good news, and I want to share it with you right away."

Tara held her breath and crossed all her fingers.

"Mr. Winsor just told me that the school board has reversed its decision." She ran her long fingers through her curly hair. "I'll be here next year after all. I want you all to come back and visit me then!"

Richard whistled. "This calls for a celebration!"

He dug around in his desk and pulled out a ten-pack of chewing gum. Bowing low, he presented Miss Dalton with a stick of grape, then paraded up and down the aisles handing out various flavors.

When Miss Dalton unwrapped her chewing gum and popped it in her mouth, the kids did the same. Soon smacks, chews, and chomps filled the air.

Peter drew a snake tattoo on his muscle with purple magic marker. "What made those buzzards change their minds, Miss Dalton?" he asked.

Their teacher rested against the corner of her desk. "After your great support, the board went back to next year's budget and decided to cut out some other things."

"Like what?" Amber asked. "I was afraid to ask my dad about it."

"Well, rather than buy a new school bus, we'll make

do with that old rattletrap one more year. And replacing the auditorium seats at the high school has been postponed." She slipped on her sweater. "Also plans for a bigger computer for the library were put on hold."

"But you're staying," Tara said. "That's the main thing."

"Thanks to you kids," Miss Dalton said. "By the way, next year I'll just teach sixth grade part-time—the science and social studies sections. The rest of the day I'll run the media center, so drop in there sometime."

Tara leaned back, weak with relief as she blew a huge green bubble. Grinning, Karin reached over and flattened it.

That day after school, Tara left after Amber was picked up for her voice lesson. Halfway home, she remembered the English book she'd left on her desk. On Monday Miss Button planned a test on diagramming sentences. Irritated with herself, she turned around.

Back at school, Tara spotted Miss Dalton coming out of the restroom. She'd changed into blue jeans and a plaid flannel shirt and was pulling on some flowered work gloves.

"What are you doing?" Tara asked, meeting her at the door to the classroom.

"Remember all those little evergreens we planted last month to start a windbreak? I'm going to water them before I go home." She put her arm around Tara and winked. "If you're *dying* for something to do, I bet the janitor has two buckets."

Tara laughed. "Sure, I'll help water." It would be great to have Miss Dalton to herself for a while.

Five minutes later they were behind the school, filling two buckets from the outdoor spigot. They gave each small evergreen half a bucket of water. The windbreak was part of a science project their class had done after studying soil erosion. Some day, the trees would cut the wind that howled across the field behind the school during the winter.

"Where'd you get these trees?" Tara asked, watering her fourth six-inch-tall tree.

"From the state nursery. When I explained what I wanted the trees for, they donated all thirty of them." She turned her empty bucket upside down, sat on it, and gasped dramatically. "Let's break for a minute. I'm not as young as you are."

Tara sat cross-legged on the grass. Although she wouldn't admit it, her arms ached too. "Miss Dalton, can I ask you something?"

"Sure."

"Why do you do so many things outside of school hours with us? Like planting these trees on a Saturday, or helping us to do the play?"

Miss Dalton rubbed her cheek with her work glove,

leaving a muddy streak. "I guess I think of you kids as my family."

"But you're so pretty. Don't you want to get married and have your own kids?"

Miss Dalton stared across the open field. Tara's stomach churned when she didn't answer; obviously she'd asked a question that was too personal.

"I'm sorry." Tara stood and brushed off her jeans. "You don't have to answer."

"No, I don't mind." Miss Dalton stood too and picked up her bucket. "You just caught me by surprise. You see, I *was* married once. A long time ago. We even had a baby girl."

Tara fell into step beside her teacher. "What was her name?"

"Beth, and she was beautiful. She died suddenly just after her first birthday." Miss Dalton squatted beside the spigot and let the water run full force. "The house was too empty for my husband after that, and he finally left. So now you kids are my family."

Tara didn't know what to say. Miss Dalton talked so matter-of-factly about it, as if it had happened to someone else. "I'm sorry about your little girl," she finally mumbled.

"Thank you." Side by side, they carried four more buckets of water to the trees. "Got any big plans for the weekend?" Miss Dalton finally asked.

"I think I'll go skating tomorrow. I haven't gone in a long time."

"Me either. Maybe I'll go too." She poured her water slowly, waiting as it soaked into the ground before pouring more. "Maybe we could skate couples again. I'll try to stay on my feet this time."

"Even if we fall down again, that's okay." Tara nodded firmly. "You don't have to skate perfectly to have a good time."

"True." Miss Dalton emptied her bucket, then rubbed her back tiredly. "Guess we're done for now. Thanks so much for helping. Meet you at the rink after lunch tomorrow?"

"I'd like that." Tara glanced down the row of tiny evergreens, then up into her teacher's face. "I'd like that a whole lot."